Claims,
How To Collect Insurance Money Without a Lawyer

By
Gordon Smith

Cargo Publishing Company
Houston, Texas

Dedication

This book is dedicated to the memory of **George W. Howell**, adjuster, husband, father and friend. He instigated the writing of this book, read the early manuscript and made suggestions for some of the revisions. George died recently while on a trip to France. I am in his debt for suggesting and encouraging the creation of the book. His optimism and excitement came through to me in a very special way. I shall always miss our long leisurely talks together.

gs

Table of Contents

(Contents Cont'd)

1 Lawyers, who needs 'em?

How would you react if I were to ask you to give me half of your money? I think most strongly that you would say no.

Ok, what if I were to ask you to give me a third of your money, wouldn't you surely still say: "NO?" I'm sure you would, but it puzzles me to contemplate the fact that you might be giving away at least one-third or more of your money to a lawyer for doing something for you which *you can easily do for yourself.*

Giving away money is giving away money. Any time you pay someone else to perform some service for you which you can and probably should do for yourself, YOU ARE GIVING MONEY AWAY!

America's Favorite Charity

In today's world, more often than not, people involved in car accidents hire lawyers to help them collect money from insurance companies. They don't always need a lawyer, and after they hire the lawyer, the lawyer usually winds up getting more money for himself than he gets for his client. Why is that so? Well, it comes from the method of payment to the lawyer. You see, lawyers don't always ask for their fee or any part of it up front. Especially in cases of claims against insurance companies, they usually work on a "contingency fee" basis. That simply means that the lawyer will handle the claim, collect the money if possible and take his fee as a share of the amount the insurance company pays you. These fees start at 33 percent and range as high as 45 percent in normal accident cases.

And that's not the end of it. There are expenses involved in the handling of a claim. Every minute the lawyer works on your claim, his clock is running as well as the clocks of those with whom he must deal. There are investigators' fees, document copying fees, fees to hospitals, to records departments such as police and other government agencies and even fees, rather large fees, paid to doctors for their reports. Most of the fees are totally unnecessary, but they sure do add up! By the time you get your share, your recovery from the insurance can be reduced by 50 percent! That's half of YOUR money! If you do the work yourself, you will avoid most of those "fees" and you will get to keep all of the money you collect from the insurance company for YOURSELF.

How about the length of time it takes to collect that money? If you think that having a lawyer handle the claim for you will get the money in your hands sooner, think again. It normally takes from three months to several years for a lawyer to collect insurance money for you. "Why," you say? Because of a number of things. For one, every time a lawyer gets involved, the claim becomes more difficult to handle for the insurance company and its adjuster. The adjuster can no longer deal directly with you. In fact, he can't even talk to you about the claim, and little of anything else, once you have hired an attorney to represent you. Everything must go through the lawyer and it is not in the lawyer's best interest to do anything in a hurry.

The lawyer's job is to collect as much money as possible on the claim because his fee will be based on how much he collects. If he collects more money from the insurance company, he gets to keep more for himself as his fee. Getting more money from an insurance company is neither quick nor easy. Therefore, you will be left waiting much longer to get your money than you would be had you not hired the lawyer at all.

You should know that I am not now, nor have I ever been a lawyer. And, since I do not have a license to practice law, I cannot give you legal advice. It would be against the law for me to do that. Guess who passed that law?

Well, that's not all. I am not a doctor, either. I don't have a license to practice medicine. I am not a chiropractor, or any other kind of physician. So, I can't give you medical advice. (The lawyers helped with that law, too.)

I'll tell you what I am. I am an insurance adjuster. For the past 34 years, I have earned my living handling insurance claims. I have worked as a staff adjuster for insurance companies. I have worked as a claim supervisor and special investigator. I worked as an independent field adjuster and for most of the last 20 years I have owned and operated my own independent adjusting firm. I have taught and trained many adjusters who are today still employed by insurance companies and independent firms routinely handling insurance claims of all kinds.

I'll tell you what else I am. I am, and have been in the past, a victim of accidents in which insurance is involved. I have tasted the worst of what the industry has to offer. I have tried to let the insurance companies handle the matter for me and I have resorted to seeking the help of lawyers to get money for me. I have lost at both efforts. That's right. In spite of what I knew about the claim business, I lost because I did not follow a plan. I did not let the principles of collecting insurance money guide me. I simply started out thinking like an ordinary citizen and acting like one, and therefore I failed to collect the money that I deserved.

You know, it's bad enough to be ignored or mistreated by an insurance company because you are an ordinary citizen and probably don't know better. It is possible for you to be mistreated, maltreated and ignored by insurance companies *simply because* of who you are or what kind of work you do. Be careful when telling people what you do if the work you are in happens to be related in some way to the insurance industry especially if you happen to be *an adjuster.* Find out as soon as possible if the adjuster shows any sign of a prejudice against the work you do, whatever the job. And, although I wish that it were not so, there is still enough racial, ethnic, sex and age prejudices out there to thoroughly stifle communication and make your claim much more difficult to handle.

Should you encounter such prejudice, be careful. Make sure your suspicions are correct before accusing someone of it and ask to speak to that person's supervisor. Be careful and be discreet. Explain your feelings to the supervisor and allow them an opportunity to check it out for themselves. Unfortunately, if the response you get simply denies the possibility of prejudice, go on with your dealings with them until something else happens to make you believe that it is happening. At that point, should it occur, ask to speak to the claim manager. You might even want to suggest that a different adjuster be assigned to your case to help ease your concerns about the matter. If you are polite and thoughtful in your presentation, no claim manager should be reluctant to reassign your file.

I have seen how a person can fail at collecting perfectly valid claims by not knowing how to handle it themselves. And I have seen how a person can be deprived of money they rightfully have coming to them by permitting someone else to handle the claim for them. I think that I have information which will help you whether you use the services of a lawyer or not. And the key to success in collecting insurance money is to have an informed plan and follow it faithfully.

Now, I've already told you what I'm not. Not a lawyer, not a doctor and so forth. I've now told you part of who I am. An adjuster, trainer, speaker, teacher. But I'm something else as well. America is still a free country. We still have free speech, in spite of what many politicians would like to do to our Constitution. And I, like you, still enjoy my right of free speech and I am allowed to EXPRESS MY OPINIONS AND BELIEFS.

I can share with you everything I have learned over the years about what it takes to collect money from insurance companies. Along the way you are going to learn to understand many of the terms of the language of insurance - the jargon used by the people in the industry. You will be able to talk intelligently and knowingly with adjusters, lawyers, doctors, wrecker drivers, nurses, body shop repairmen, police officers, investigators, claim supervisors, paralegals and claim managers.

You will learn to identify "runners," very important members of the lawyer's unofficial staff. You are going to learn what to look for, what to gather up and how to present the information to the proper parties which will result in the best recovery possible for you.

If you handle the claim for yourself, the total amount you collect will vary. It might be less than what the lawyer would have collected, but the amount of money you get to keep for yourself will be greater in most cases than what you might have kept under the same circumstances except for having to share your money with a lawyer. How do I know this? During my career in insurance claims, I have been privy to the inside information of the insurance companies. I know how much the companies have been willing to pay for claims over the years regardless of whether the claimants were represented by a lawyer or not. A value is assigned to each claim based on certain factors such as medical bills, lost wages and such. Often it has nothing whatsoever to do with the lawyer. And a very high percentage of the claims are settled for about the amount so determined by the insurance company.

Furthermore, each insurance policy has a maximum limit of money it will pay out. It's called the *Policy Limits.* If your claim has a value which is greater than the maximum amount of the policy limit, the insurance company will pay no more than that amount. The lawyer can't do anything about it as far as the insurance company is concerned. There are other ways to go about recovering excess amounts, but we will discuss that later. For the moment, consider that the lawyer is representing you on a claim, that your claim is worth more that what the insurance company CAN pay. The company would pay you that amount whether you are represented by a lawyer or not. What I'm saying is that often the lawyer is only in the claim for his share of your money, which means you could have gotten ALL of the money for yourself without a lawyer.

When I say that the lawyer gets his fee as a share of your money, bear in mind that I'm also saying that the lawyer gets **nothing**, if **you** get nothing. Most Personal Injury attorneys get paid only if they succeed in collecting an insurance claim for their clients. The lawyers MUST COLLECT or they get nothing for all their time and energy. As you can see, the lawyer has an enormous incentive to succeed in collecting the claim for you. It would be unrealistic to think that anyone alive today is perfect. That includes lawyers. Because they are imperfect, we can expect them to do things which may not be exactly right. May not be exactly ethical. May not be exactly LEGAL. It is reasonable to assume the possibility that in responding to so much pressure to collect, some lawyers might be tempted to step over some prohibited lines in order to get the money.

The insurance companies and adjusters are very much aware of this. Part of their job is to make every reasonable effort to prevent anyone from collecting more than they deserve. Part of their job is to watch the lawyers closely, to see to it as far as they can that the lawyers are not allowed to cheat or to fudge or to commit criminal acts in their effort to collect insurance money. All of this means that the claim process is almost always slowed down the moment a lawyer gets involved. It means that the claim process is almost always made much more costly to the insurance industry. It almost always means that your insurance rates and mine will go higher next year because of the increased cost of handling claims, solely because lawyers get involved.

Lawyers make a lot of money. Do you know how much money insurance lawyers (they are called "plaintiff lawyers" in the industry) get paid for handling claims against insurance companies? In some cases the amounts are staggering! Even those lawyers who are not very good at what they do - even those lawyers who are not very smart or productive - earn incomes far higher than what ordinary folks get paid for what they do. And the good ones - the bright, aggressive, ambitious lawyers - believe me, they make the sort of yearly income that most of us only dream about.

Sure, there are many levels of lawyers. There are those who become very well off, but not "filthy rich." But there are some lawyers in this country who have collected as their share of insurance payments so much money that they have become untouchable. They are not only free of the pain of not having enough money to satisfy their needs and wants, but sometimes find themselves above even the law itself. They become immune because of the amount of money they have gathered up by handling insurance claims for people like you.

OK, so what? I could go on and on about how much money lawyers make, but so what? Is there anything wrong with lawyers making that much money? Well, let me ask you this: "Would there be anything wrong with you making that much money?" Absolutely not! And there is nothing wrong with lawyers making that much money either. Every lawyer had to spend from 16 to 20 years in school earning a law degree. Each and every one of them had to struggle through their state's Bar examination to earn a license to practice law. My hat is off to all of them who make it through.

And for most of them, they work very hard prying money out of the hands of the insurance companies and getting that same money into the hands of their clients - - AND *into their own hands and pockets!* They earn it! If you care to check them out some holiday such as Labor Day, Memorial Day or Fourth of July, you may find them in their offices, maybe in their jogging shorts or golf shirts, but there at the office working on ways and means of collecting money from insurance companies. When they do, they earn their money. My question is whether it is necessary for them to be involved at all. In most cases, I think not.

Let's talk numbers. Let's imagine that you have a claim against someone who is insured by some big insurance company and, considering everything, your claim is worth $100,000. Let's say that the insurance company agrees as to the fact that they owe you the money and that the amount they owe is $100,000. If the attorney collects that $100,000, the first thing to come out is the attorney's share or $33,000! Remember, that's not all. There are expenses as well, and in a case worth $100,000, there will be plenty of expenses. You could expect to see as much as $5,000 to $10,000 more taken out for expenses.

Don't forget good ole' Doc Whatizname who wrote all those twenty-six page reports for your lawyer to send to the insurance company. My guess is that he and the other medical providers will get another $25,000 to $30,000 , bringing total deductions to a whopping **$73,000!** Possibly. I can't say for sure, since this is guestimating. But I think you get the point. Your $100,000 settlement could easily be reduced to only $27,000 long before you ever see a penny of it.

I must hasten to add that there are other problems involved as well. There is no way in this world that you or anyone else is ever going to collect $100,000 from an insurance company unless you are very seriously injured or unless you play the game to the hilt. That means you must at least take off work for extended periods of time. Well, if you're not employed anyway, I guess that's OK. But what if you have a job, a good job, which you like and want to keep? You can't be taking off work much and keep the job as well. And if you don't take off work, the lawyer will not be able to convince the insurance company that your claim is worth $100,000. If you do take off, you will probably, if you are like most of us, not get paid. You will have to get money to survive from some place.

Well, that's another problem. Where do you get survival money - living expenses? In spite of the fact that it is illegal for a lawyer to finance your claim, they do it anyway. Oh, not all of them, but a large enough number that it continues to regularly and significantly contribute to the problems of the insurance industry and to ever-increasing costs to the public as well. If the lawyer "advances" money to you, he is actually lending the money to you. What happens when you borrow money from a bank or get your car financed by a finance company? Why - you have to pay it back. And pay it back to the lawyer you must as well.

Depending upon how long it takes for your lawyer to collect this $100,000, how much money do you think you might have to borrow? If it takes a year or more to collect the settlement, you are going to be deeply in debt to your lawyer before you get through and that debt must be paid out of the remaining $27,000 which you thought you were going to get! That $100,000 settlement and collection from the insurance company doesn't look so good now, does it? Should it cost that much? I don't know. I know if the lawyer works for you, he is entitled to get paid. If the doctor works for you, he is entitled to get paid. Anyone else who spends their professional time assisting you in collecting from an insurance company deserves to get paid for their services and that is your cost of using their services in the first place.

Is it necessary for you to give up such a large portion of your claim payment just to collect it? The answer, in most cases, is a resounding **NO!**

But wait! Does every insurance claim get paid? Sorry. I'm afraid not. Some claims never get paid. Why? Because they are not owed. There are many reasons claims have to be paid and there are also many reasons why the insurance companies can legitimately refuse payment of any kind. If the insurance company <u>does not owe the money</u>, the claim will be denied. In most of such cases there is not much the lawyer can do about it. You see, what I'm saying is that usually when a lawyer collects an insurance claim, it is a claim which the insurance company <u>would have paid in any case</u>. And <u>often</u>, the payment is for no more with an attorney than it is without.

The insurance companies are not being run by fools! If a claimant hires a lawyer, the insurance company hires a lawyer, too. They must. The insurance policy promises you as a policyholder that if you get sued for any reason covered by the insurance policy, the company will provide and pay for a lawyer to defend you. These lawyers are called "defense attorneys." So if you have a claim against someone else who is insured and you hire a lawyer to represent you, the company must hire a lawyer to defend the person against whom you are making a claim. I'm not saying that the insurance companies automatically hire lawyers on every claim, but if your lawyer files suit, an insurance company defense attorney is hired. These defense attorneys are people who specialize in trying to prevent plaintiff attorneys from collecting money from insurance companies.

And there is no reason to think that the lawyer working against the insurance company is going to be any smarter or better than the lawyer working <u>for</u> the insurance company. There is no magic bag of tricks, no special secrets or devastating tactics known to the Personal Injury lawyers that the lawyers working for the insurance company don't also know about. After all, they all went to the same school! They belong to the same clubs. They pal around with one another. What do you expect lawyers to do? They socialize the same as doctors and mechanics, usually with friends in the same or similar job and economic circumstances.

Please believe me when I say that I have no desire to belittle, denigrate, slander or in any other way accuse lawyers of dishonesty or collusion. I only want you to understand that it is a business with them. And they are equally good on both sides of the bar, that's the bar of justice I'm talking about, not the other kind of bar. What I'm getting at here is that for the most part, lawyers want to represent you on a claim which they know they can collect! Why? Because that's how they make their money! If the lawyer is sure that he will collect, do you think that there is any valid reason why you can't collect the same claim yourself without the lawyer? If you do, then you are mistaken. Thousands of lawyers make their living collecting money from insurance companies when there is no reason whatsoever for a lawyer to be involved in the case at all! And <u>that</u> is where you come in.

2 I'm Gonna Wash That Lawyer Right Out Of My Hair.

So maybe now you are thinking that you really don't need a lawyer to collect insurance money. But then you say: "NOW you tell me! I already <u>have</u> a lawyer." Well, that doesn't mean you have to keep him. That's right. Just because you have already hired a lawyer, signed a contingency fee contract and all of that, you can still get the lawyer out of the picture, if you want to.

It is not always easy. Many times the lawyer will already have put some work into the file and he wants to get paid for it. And he should get paid for it. After all, that is what the lawyer is in business for. You know, we are all really "just in it for the money." How many days would you keep going to work if you didn't get paid for working? Not long, I'll bet. We all must eat. We all must pay rent or mortgage payments. Almost everyone now has a car and most of us must make payments on an automobile loan at a bank or finance company. Then there is the telephone bill, the electric bill, maybe a gas bill. Credit cards, charge accounts, gasoline cards, movies, cigarettes, beer coke candy popcorn toys clothes and on and on and on! IT ALL TAKES MONEY! WE ALL MUST HAVE MONEY! **WE ARE ALL IN IT FOR THE MONEY!**

So, your lawyer may - probably <u>will</u> - want to get paid for his work. Although that is not always true, it is in many cases and you must deal with it. A number of things might happen and it is important for you to be aware of them. Once you have signed a contract, (and I am assuming that your lawyer is smart enough to have written a valid one), you are obligated to him. If you want to "fire" your lawyer, many times you can only do so <u>with his permission</u>!

Fifty Ways To Leave Your Lover

Do not confuse what we are talking about here with firing a lawyer because he is incompetent, or has mistreated you or has not fulfilled his end of the contract. In those cases, more often than not, you can just bounce him out of your life. You have little to fear if he has really performed poorly, since he probably won't want to do anything about it anyway. But be extremely careful about trying to get rid of a competent attorney who is doing his job correctly and is making a good faith effort to collect money for you. In those cases, the lawyer is in the driver's seat. You can discharge him only if he agrees to it, and he is pretty much free to dictate the terms of any dissolution of your relationship with him.

Now, the good news is that many times, a lawyer doesn't want to mess with you if you do not want him representing you any longer. That relationship can become as bad as a bad marriage. If you and your lawyer "fall out of love", you might as well go ahead and get the "divorce." Your lawyer will probably agree. He cannot successfully defend a client who no longer wants his services. But still, he is entitled to be paid for what he has already done for you AND he is entitled to a share of the proceeds of your insurance claim settlement.

Remember that contract you signed? Well, whether you remember it or not, and I have met many people who had no memory of it at all, the lawyer won't forget it. That piece of paper is the only thing which makes it possible for the lawyer to collect any money at all, for you or for himself. When you hire a lawyer, you ask him to legally speak for you, to stand in your place. You ask him to be as you are to the extent you authorize him to act in your behalf. That piece of paper - the contract - is the lawyer's legal proof of that fact that you want him to act and speak for you. It is also his proof that he has a right to get paid. If you later decide that you wish to get out of your agreement with the lawyer, the lawyer has a right to ask for payment of any sum he thinks will adequately compensate him for the work he has already done.

What are some of the possibilities? Well, to begin with, your lawyer might just let you go!

That's right, he may just say: "To heck with it" and let you out of the agreement. Usually this occurs when your claim has little value anyway. Often it occurs just because the attorney's volume of business is so great that he doesn't really care about your one claim. Sometimes he hasn't been able to get any work done on the file and reasonably agrees that you owe him nothing. Sometimes, and this one warms the cockles of any adjuster's heart, the client may have asked the lawyer to represent him on a claim which is totally without merit and the adjuster can prove it! In these cases, you don't usually have to ask the lawyer to let you out of the contract, he lets you out! This can work in your favor if you have been less than honest with your attorney and want to get rid of him. You only need to let him know of your "deception" and if he is a reputable attorney, he will probably not want to represent you any longer.

Whatever the reason, if the attorney is willing to let you go without demanding payment of any kind or a share in the proceeds of your claim, count your blessings and get out while you can.

Pay Me Now Or . . .

But if your attorney is not so generous, you will be faced with some of the other possibilities. The lawyer may just ask you for a fee. The fee can range anywhere from his minimum charge to a substantial sum of money, depending upon two factors: (1) How much work he already has done on the file; and (2) How much he thinks your claim is ultimately worth.

As for minimum charges, they are like spring flowers - they are all over the place. It is hard to imagine an attorney willing to accept less than $100 for any service at all. So, you can more than likely expect to be asked for at least that much. The upper limit? I don't know. You can probably make a pretty good guess at it yourself, depending upon how much you know about your claim. And after you get through with this book, you should be able to place a value on the claim yourself, and therefore you should also be able to guess fairly accurately as to the fee your lawyer is likely to ask to let go of your contract.

Bear in mind that if the lawyer continues working for you and successfully collects insurance money for you, he will be entitled to at least one-third. Of course that would mean he would have to do more work on the file. If there remains much to be done, you should argue your position strongly with the lawyer, pointing out to him how little has been done to date and how much remains to be done before anyone will get any money. And remember: NEGOTIATE! That's how the lawyer gets money in the first place and it is how you can improve your position with him. Everything, - and I mean EVERYTHING - is negotiable.

Or Pay Me Later

If your lawyer has already completed a substantial amount of work on the file or if there is very little left of what had to be done in the first place, he will not be willing to settle for a flat fee, certainly not a modest one. If your claim has substantial value, believe me your lawyer is not going to easily let go of a lucrative contract. In these cases, he will assuredly want to retain his equity in your claim settlement. That simply means that he won't let you out of the contract unless you agree to pay him the agreed upon contingency fee set forth in your contract with him.

Now, you may be thinking: "Well, what would I want to do that for?" Good question. At this point you must decide for yourself whether you want to continue with the attorney or not. If you get out of the contract, but your lawyer retains a one-third interest in your settlement, you may be thinking: "Why not let him do all the work?" Believe it or not, there may be good reason.

Remember those expenses we talked about earlier? If your lawyer, in making his effort to collect the money for you, has retained or has in mind retaining certain doctors for the purpose of testifying about your medical condition - doctors he knows will be instrumental in making your claim look much more dangerous and therefore valuable to the insurance company than it might otherwise appear - the cost of those doctors will be great. If he has in mind sending you for expensive diagnostic testing, testing which you may or may not need, the bills are going to soar! EVERY PENNY COMES OUT OF YOUR SHARE OF THE SETTLEMENT, not his. There are other expenses and delays which can result in reducing the ultimate net amount of the insurance money which you get to keep for yourself.

Too Late Now

On the other hand, if you've already gone through the mill, seen all the doctors, taken all the tests, run up all the expenses needed to push the claim to its ultimate limit in the judgement of your lawyer, you might just as well leave it with him. There will be little for you to gain in such circumstances. Don't under any circumstances start to think that you are smarter than the lawyer, because you probably are not. You may be more intelligent, but your lawyer has the training and the experience. So don't consider getting rid of your lawyer for any flimsy reasons. Think it through and take such action only when it makes a substantial difference in the money you get to keep.

Finally, what if the attorney just says no? Maybe he has been listening to the anti-drug commercials and can't get the phrase out of his head. What if he just won't let you out of the contract at all? You need to try to figure out why he would take such a position. Actually he can't force you to continue with the contract against your will, but he has every right to enforce those provisions of the contract which benefit him if you insist on letting him go. But if he tells you that he will not let you out of the contract under any circumstances, ask him to explain why. It's really just that simple. Just ask: "Why?"

Kiss And Make Up

He will tell you in one way or another. Surprise, surprise, it may be in your best interest! He is after all a lawyer and might be able to show you where you are truly better off being represented. The test is to find out if he thinks you would be better off being represented by a lawyer, even if you decided the lawyer should be someone other than him. If he can honestly tell you that, then give it some further thought. But be careful. Don't let the lawyer "con" you into staying with him solely for his financial gain alone. If the lawyer can't convince you that he is being honest and is speaking in your best interest, he may just be being a jerk about it. I mean he may just be angry because you are taking the claim away from him and thereby depriving him of some money.

In that case, talk to him calmly and reasonably. Explain why you want to handle the claim on your own. Don't be afraid to tell him that you think that you will wind up keeping more of the settlement if you do it on your own. If you were "led" to the lawyer or in anyway talked into hiring him in the first place, tell him of your discomfort and regret. If he will still not let you out, consider anything at all unusual about the way you arrived at dealing with this attorney in the first place. You may recall something about the transaction which the attorney would not want you talking with someone else about. You must be tactful in the way you present such information, but hey, you're already in a jam with him, so work it out.

There are some cases where you cannot get out of the contract and some cases where it would make no sense for you to make any change. In that case, relax and let the claim run its course. Study this book to educate yourself so you can keep a watchful eye on the attorney as he continues. He may make a mistake. You will want to be able to catch it if it should happen, especially after trying to get out and having been refused. Wouldn't that be embarrassing?

3 Where do we go from here?

Ok, so you have no lawyer. You either never hired one or you have gotten rid of the one you had. So, where do you go from here? What's next? First, it is a good idea to begin at the beginning. The beginning of every insurance claim is an accident or loss of some kind. Let's begin there - at the accident. Oh, by the way, is there a time when you really need a lawyer? Yes, there most definitely is, but we will get to that later on. But, if you are as anxious to read this book as I am to write it, we need to get on with it.

The Accident.

It is important for you to understand that accidents are all alike. Now wait a minute! Here is what happens: Somebody does something and the result of what they did was not what they intended it to be or not what they expected it to be. That's all there is to it. Well, sure there are the details of your particular accident, but the basics are the same. One or more people arrive at the same place in space and time and do something they should not do or fail to do something they should have done. When these elements all fall together, something unexpected and unintended takes place. That something is called an accident.

All accidents are different. (What? I thought you said . . .) Yes, they are all the same and yet they are all different. Different in the exact facts of any particular accident. The facts of your accident are extremely important to the matter of whether you can collect insurance money or not. You need to learn how to see your accident through the eyes of a stranger, someone who was not there at the time it occurred, in order that you will be able to describe it in detail to the agent, adjuster, investigator or other person involved in making the decision to pay you money or not pay you money.

You may have heard it said that if your car gets hit from behind, the person driving the car who hit you is automatically at fault and owes for the damage to your car. That is exactly what has happened in so many cases in the past that the "old wives' tale" grew out of those cases. Nevertheless, it is not always true. The point is that it is very important that you know, understand and remember the facts, the true facts, of your particular accident. And I believe that best way to do that is to write it down as soon as possible after the accident.

I realize that if you or someone close to you has been injured in an accident, you will most certainly want to see to it that all injured parties get medical attention as soon as possible. If your car is not driveable, you will want to take care of having it moved to a garage or other repair or storage facility and you may be required to spend some time with the police. But as soon as possible, the first thing to do after the accident is to sit down with paper and pen and write down everything you remember about the accident. Write it all down. No one will get to read those notes but you, so say whatever you want to. Write down all your thoughts and feelings, impressions and beliefs, and facts - TRUE facts for future reference.

Some of the facts you know or remember might not be favorable to your side of the accident, but in this exercise you should only be concerned with the truth. If the truth hurts you, write it down anyway, we will deal with it later on. As you will be learning later on, you don't have to tell anybody everything. The insurance company representative will be working hard enough to uncover information which will prevent you from collecting insurance money. You don't need to help them any. Remember, your object is to collect money, not to render justice. Justice is a moral concept. If the facts are against you and your conscience won't let you attempt to collect money from someone else, Hooray for you! I mean that in all sincerity. If you are wrong and are honest enough to admit it, at least to yourself, you are one of the rare people on this earth whom the rest of us should admire greatly. But if you are like most of us, you will probably want to withhold some information about your accident, leaving those details for someone else to uncover.

Justice Is Blind . . . Or Stupid!

If you are wondering if there is anything wrong with that, please understand that in the American judicial system we go at each other on an adversarial basis. That simply means that each side is always trying to beat the other side and to win for itself. The police arrest someone for a crime. That person hires a lawyer for defense. The city, county, state or national government hires a lawyer, called a prosecutor, to prosecute the charges against the accused. Each lawyer goes into court with one goal in mind - to WIN! The prosecutor wants to win by getting a conviction and sending the accused to jail. The defense lawyer wants to win to get his client excused from the charges and set free.

If you think for one minute that those lawyers, the judge or anyone else involved in that trial is trying to find or prove "Justice", you are sadly mistaken. The lawyers are trying to win. The judge is trying to make sure the lawyers follow the rules and if there is a jury involved, they are told what to do by the judge. They often render verdicts which are contrary to what they would decide if justice were the only issue. You see, the juries also must follow the rules and they can't always do what they would like to do.

Therefore, if you are going to play the game, you need to understand the rules also. And the first rule is: "Try to win." Whenever a person is involved in a dispute involving a matter which is covered by an insurance policy, they must organize their resources and plan their strategies to take action which will lead to victory, not justice. For if you work for justice and the other side is working toward your defeat, how much chance do you really think you have? So, I say, **Learn which facts you should tell and which you should keep to yourself.**

It's A Sin To Tell A Lie

DO NOT ASSUME THAT ANY SUGGESTION IS BEING MADE HERE FOR YOU TO LIE! **DO NOT LIE!** You <u>must</u> tell the truth. If you start lying or deliberately misleading people, there is a great probability that you will get caught. You will collect no insurance money and you might even be charged with a crime yourself.

This is probably a good point at which to explain some basic law. When a person "breaks the law" and gets arrested, he is charged with committing a "Crime." A crime is committed when a person intentionally violates a law which provides penalties such as fines and serving time in jail. His offense is said to be against the people of the community. Therefore, you will read about, hear about and sometimes see on television, cases known as: "The People against John Doe;" or "The State against John Doe;" or, maybe: "The Commonwealth against John Doe." In these cases, the prosecuting lawyer is hired by the government. The person charged with the crime must defend himself from attack by the government trying to enforce its laws.

There is another kind of offense which is not a crime in the sense that the government is not involved as a party to the lawsuit. Technically they are called "torts," but don't worry about what they are called. They are actually "Civil Wrongs" as compared to "Criminal Wrongs." You cannot be sent to jail for a tort. You cannot, at least in the usual sense, be fined for a civil wrong. But you can, however, be sued by a fellow citizen.

Here is what can happen. First of all, it is important for you to understand about the duties we owe to one another. The law, through the courts in England and the United States, has evolved into a set of rules which govern the conduct of people living with and around each other called the "Common Law." The Common Law is created by what judges have to say in their legal opinions. Try to remember that the laws of a country are supposed to be written by the legislature, not the judges. But as the judges make decisions, other courts follow these decisions and the decision itself becomes a sort of law. Most of the common law concerns itself with the obligations we have to each other as citizens.

Rules To Live By

I have a duty to not hit you. You have a duty not to ride my horse without my permission. A stranger who comes into our community has a duty to stay out of our yards, fields and homes. If any of us breaks these rules, we have committed a civil wrong or a tort. Now, since the government doesn't really give a damn what we do to one another generally, unless we break one of the government's rules, the government will not bother to hire a prosecutor to bring the perpetrator to "justice." If anyone is going to make the offender "pay" for his transgression, it is up to the "injured" person to "prosecute."

Being injured does not necessarily mean "bodily injury." It really means "damages." And "damages" really means dollars and cents. In other words, the hurt done to someone which can be measured in money. You have been damaged if your property has been broken or used without your permission. You may have been damaged if someone enters upon your land without your permission. You can claim damages for someone telling lies about you. You have a right to "prosecute" someone for causing you to lose money in your business under some circumstances. Of course, you have also been damaged if your body itself is harmed in some way.

You are the injured party if any of these things happen to you, among many others. The key point here is that in order for you to be able to punish a person for doing any of these things to you, you must prove that the person failed to live up to his obligation to you. In other words that he "breached a duty owed" to you and that his breach of duty caused your damages. You must also prove that you didn't do anything to cause the damage yourself.

This breach of a duty or failure to observe the common law rules governing our conduct is regarded as negligence. Remember what we said about a crime? That the act is intentional? The government, in order to prove a crime, must prove the accused person intended to break the law. In prosecuting civil wrongs it is not necessary to prove intent. In fact, most such incidents are truly accidental. But even though it is an accident, if the acts which led up to the accident can be called "a breach of a duty owed," the person can be held responsible.

An automobile accident. One person is driving a car on a public street, runs a stop sign and collides with another car traveling on the cross street. The driver of the car which ran the stop sign had a duty to the driver and owner of the other car to not run the stop sign. He had a duty to stop his car at the stop sign and allow the other driver to pass by safely. In not stopping, the offending driver breached a duty which he owed to the driver of the car on the cross street. Based on these facts, it can be shown that the damage to the car on the cross street and any bodily injury done to its driver are the result of the first driver's failure to stop at the stop sign.

The first driver was careless or negligent, he broke the rules which require him to let the other traffic go by ahead of him and he damaged other people. That is a tort. It is a civil wrong and is punishable. Typically, the method of punishment is to make the perpetrator of this wrong pay money to the person damaged. This is called "paying damages."

You may be thinking: "Hey, wait a minute. Didn't that guy break a law, too? Didn't he run the stop sign? Shouldn't he get a ticket?" Yep! You're right. That is a crime. It can be prosecuted as a crime and the "criminal" could be forced to pay a fine to the government as his punishment. But you don't get any of that. So, if you want to collect money for these damages, you must file a civil action against the "perp." (That's TV talk for perpetrator.) You do that by first making a claim against the person and, failing to collect that way, by filing a lawsuit against him. Want to know something else? You don't always need a lawyer to make a claim or file a lawsuit either. You can probably easily see how you might not need a lawyer to file a claim, but a lawsuit? That's right. In some cases you don't even need a lawyer for that. (Think: "Small Claims Court.")

The Wheels Of Justice

One more thing before we get away from this lecture on the law. In order for the courts to hold a person responsible for his negligent acts or his negligent failure to act, two other things must be shown. The first is that the damages complained of are the "proximate" result of the perpetrator's negligence. The second is that in order to be proven negligent, the perpetrator must fracture the so-called "Reasonable Man" rule. (I guess now days they call it the "Reasonable Person" rule)

Many years ago, the courts tried to settle the question of what amounts to negligence. They decided that if a person did what a fictional <u>reasonable</u> person would do, his conduct would not be called negligent - at least not in the eyes of the law. They decided that if a person did not act in such a way as this fictional *reasonable* person would likely act, he would be regarded as having been negligent. Sound complicated? Well, it can be. But don't worry about it. If you get caught up in an issue as complicated as this, you will probably already have a lawyer anyway. Just bear in mind that if in your judgment a person did what you might have done under the same or similar circumstances, he might not be found negligent.

Okay, what about "proximate?" Am I trying to say "approximately" and just not getting it right? NO. "Proximate" is another "legalese" word that you will never use unless you are talking with a lawyer or discussing a civil lawsuit. However, it might be useful for you to understand a little of what it means. First, it does not mean that something happened *approximately* because of something else. That would mean that it *almost* caused something to happen. Or that it *nearly* caused something to happen. Proximate means that one thing occurred *only* because of another thing. You might think of it as a "direct" cause or an event which is directly linked to the result. That is not totally correct or at least not the complete description of proximate, but it is *approximately* what proximate means. It means, in short, that you must prove that your damages are the result of another person's acts, not just that your damage occurred at a time when another person did something else.

If you can prove the other party "negligent" and that your damages are the "proximate" result of his negligence, you can make him pay you for your loss. If you can't, you lose.

What has all of this to do with collecting insurance money? You see, the insurance company is not liable to you in an accident. The person who hurts you is the party who may be liable. But if that person has a policy of liability insurance which covers the incident, the insurance will step in to pay any money the other guy owes you. Once again, the insurance company will not pay you because the insurance company owes you. They will only pay if they insure someone else who owes you.

So, you must prove the other guy negligent. You must prove that you were damaged. You must prove that your damages were caused by the other guy's negligence and you need to show that you are an innocent lamb. AND, the other guy better have some liability insurance to cover his negligence or there will be no question of collecting insurance money. Of course, if the guy who hurts you has money or property of his own, you may be able to collect your money damages directly from him. But, well, in today's world, that is highly unlikely. If the guy is rich, okay, but if he is just an ordinary fellow like most of us, you won't stand much of a chance of getting paid.

But if he has insurance, now we got a ball game! THE FACTS OF YOUR ACCIDENT ARE THE ENTIRE BASIS OF PROVING ALL THESE THINGS YOU HAVE JUST READ ABOUT! That is why it is so important for you to write down the details of your accident as soon as possible after it occurs. It is important to be as complete as possible. It is important to be honest with yourself. And it is important to write it all down. Soon. No, <u>sooner</u> than that.

4 Facts and Figures.

The most important things you need to know about any accident include the following: Where was each party immediately prior to the accident? What was each person doing? Where was each person going? If they were moving, in which direction were they moving? What was each person attempting to do? What did each person do? What was the result of what each did? What exactly happened? After the "happening", where did each person go and what happened to them then? Where did each person wind up after the accident was over? What were the consequences of the events of the accident?

The World In Review

To get to all of this information in proper order, it is sometimes helpful to begin by describing the scene where the accident occurred. When talking about an automobile accident, you start by naming and describing the streets on which it occurred. Make a note of or find out the exact name of the street. Answer these questions if you can: How wide is the street? You can say it is so many feet wide if you like, but it is better to describe it in terms of how many driving lanes it has. Include all of the lanes. In other words, if it is a narrow street with only one lane going in each direction, call it a "two-lane" street. If it has two lanes going in each direction, call it a "four lane" street, and so forth. Is it a paved road? Concrete, asphalt, gravel, dirt? Was it in good condition? Was there any construction going on in the street? What is the speed limit on that street? Was the street dry or was it wet? Okay, now how about the other street?

You should, if there is more than one street involved, give the same information for each street. Don't forget about private driveways and unnamed roads or alleys. Describe them as well. Of course, if there is more than one street involved, it is very probable that the two streets cross each other or run into each other in some way forming an *intersection.* Describe the intersection and show which directions each street runs according to the compass. The street runs north and south, or east and west, or northeast and southwest and so on. And the most important feature of any intersection is if and how the traffic going through the intersection is controlled.

The intersection might have no traffic controls at all. Such an intersection would be called and "open" or "uncontrolled" intersection. It might have Stop signs, Yield Right-Of-Way signs or Electric Traffic Signal lights. There may be other signs telling people about to enter the intersection who is allowed to go first and who is not. If there are traffic controls present, could they be clearly seen? Check the trees, bushes, signs, poles, buildings and other objects at the scene to see if any of them block anyone's view of the traffic control device. By the way, how was the visibility?

How well could you see things around you? Was there fog? Was it clear? Was the sun shining in your eyes? Did the smog make if difficult to see that old lady as she stepped from the curb into the path of your car? And how was the weather? Rain? Snow? Clear skies? Clouds? Fog? (Again). Was it windy? And how heavy was the traffic?

It is difficult to describe the amount of traffic on the streets. You can say, and most people do, that the traffic was "about average" or that it was "light" or "heavy." But what do those words mean? Try to be specific. "There were a lot of cars on the street." "There were only a few vehicles on the street." "There was no one on the street except me and that little old lady who stepped from the curb!" Well, all right I'm joking now, but the point is, tell about the traffic in a way that the person listening to you can fully understand what the conditions were like.

There are other facts about the scene of the accident which you may recall and which may or may not be helpful, but write down all you can remember. If you cannot remember what you need to know, go back to the scene of the accident and make additional notes for future reference. When you have all the details of the scene of the accident down, tell about all vehicles and other objects involved in the accident.

He Had A Hot Rod Ford And A . . .

Describe the cars in as much detail as you possibly can. Try to keep it in sequence as you write it down. "A maroon 1991 Ford Crown Victoria 4-door sedan with license plate number XXX999" Or try: "A large truck and trailer. It was white and was pulling a large closed-in van. I think it was an 18-wheeler." At least give a color, a size and the kind you think it might have been. For example, you could say, the other car was a little gray car, maybe Japanese, with only two doors, but try to remember and jot down as much information as possible. License plate numbers are VERY IMPORTANT! Color and size are important, too. You will see why later on.

Cast Of Characters

Now that you have the cars down, who was driving them? Who was riding in them? How many people were in the car (very important, if you are the defendant)? Describe the people in as much detail as you can. Forget political correctness here! Were they Black? Were they Oriental? Were they Hispanic? Was the white guy fair-skinned or dark? Was the black guy fair-skinned or dark? Was the Hispanic guy . . .? Include how tall, how heavy or skinny or short. Describe the hair color, length and style, (if they had hair). Glasses, clothing, hats or any other accessories which might have been worn can help identify someone later. This is especially important if the person was a witness. What language was spoken? Remember that there are folks out there who will try to make you believe they speak no English even though they do in order to get out of talking to you.

Keep your eyes and ears open. Pay attention. If the accident has already happened by the time you read this, use your memory as best you can and ask questions of others who may have been there to fill in what you cannot remember.

It is not unusual following a two-car accident in which there was only one person in each car to be later told that one of the cars had four or five people in it. They may want to get more of any insurance money available or they may just want to try to prove their case by having many people to testify for them. That little old lady may turn up with a friend who saw everything in spite of the smog.

Alcohol, drugs, cigarettes and insanity. It is not always true that since a person had been drinking alcohol or smoking marijuana or taking pills that the accident will automatically be considered their fault. But it always looks bad! The worst case is, of course, that if the person is "drunk," "high" or "strung out." Their vision, reaction time and coordination may be so severely impaired that they should not have been operating a vehicle or even on the street in that condition. The drugs or booze could well be the only reason the accident happened.

There are many ways you can tell if a person is using any of these substances. You are probably familiar with many of them. The most common in the case of alcohol is the smell of the other person's breath. But there are other signs as well. Slurred speech, staggering, not being able to focus their eyes can all be signs of substance abuse. However, be careful! Those symptoms can also suggest a physical impairment or disability having nothing whatsoever to do with drinking or drugging. Be sure before you start making accusations, but write it all down anyway.

This Is Not A Test

While you are writing your facts, don't worry about your writing or your spelling or your grammar. Just get down as much information as you possibly can as soon as you can. If you want to clean it up later, then clean it up later, but for now just get it written down. After you have described the scene, the vehicles and objects and the people involved in the accident, "get the facts, ma'am." Now, I don't really mean for you to put off writing down the actual facts of the accident until after you have described these other things, I just want you to know that there is a logical, orderly way of describing accidents which may help you get it all written out. But the facts of the actual accident itself are by far and away the most important of all and you may even want to write them down first and then get back to your "logical, orderly" way of describing things.

You must be detailed when describing the accident. Tell where each person was. Show where each vehicle was. Draw yourself a diagram showing all the positions on it as well as picturing the scene itself. Tell what each person or vehicle was doing or attempting to do. Describe how the vehicles hit together. Use words like this: "The front of the Ford hit the rear of the Oldsmobile." Or: "The 18-wheeler hit that old lady and knocked her so high she looked like a rocket taking off!" It's okay to be colorful. Who cares? They're your notes and anything which helps you remember, works.

Tell where everyone and everything wound up after the collision or accident. If the initial impact of the collision knocked one of the vehicles into further motion following the collision, tell how far it moved and where it stopped. If a vehicle ran away from the scene following a collision, tell how fast and which direction it went. "The old lady bounced along the top of the trailer like a basketball and fell off in the street as the truck driver drove on off. I don't think he ever saw her even though her two friends were yelling and throwing their purses at the truck as it headed north on Main Street."

Guests At The Party

Make sure you include complete information about any services provided by public or private agencies at the scene of the accident. Public agencies included Police Department, Fire Department, Ambulance Services and Public Works Departments. Private agencies may include tow trucks, ambulances, hospitals, doctors, reporters and television cameramen.

The police are the most frequently seen at accidents, although they are followed in a close second by wrecker drivers. In large metropolitan communities, there are sometimes hordes of wrecker drivers who show up hoping to get to tow one of the vehicles involved in the accident to a repair or storage facility. Police, of course, are nearly always on the scene if one or more of the vehicles are disabled by the collision. The police will, in some cases, call the fire department out to wash down the streets if fuel or other fluids leak from the damaged vehicles.

And, for those poor folks hurt in the accident, usually an ambulance is called and maybe an emergency medical team as well. In cases of severe or life-threatening injuries, helicopters are called to get the injured to a hospital as quickly as possible. The list goes on and on. Lawyers have "runners" on the scene of many accidents. The newspapers, radio stations and televisions stations sometimes have reporters on the scene. Whoever is there, if you know about them or learn about them later, WRITE IT ALL DOWN.

Include as much detail as you can. Names, badge numbers, vehicle numbers, the names of the departments, names of companies and other information may prove very valuable to you later. Although there is much information here, it can be summarized as follows: "As soon as possible after the accident, write down every piece of information available to you about events both before and after the accident as well as the exact events of the accident itself." Even if the accident happened before you bought this book, write the facts down NOW!

5 Big Puddle Of Blood

Remember that song? "There was blood on the saddle. An' blood on the ground. An' a big puddle of blood all around?" Or something like that. I hope that as you read this book you don't have to remember a scene from your accident as grisly as the one described in that song, but many accidents do produce severe and horrible injuries. They are not fun to experience, to remember or to talk about, for most people. But knowing about injuries to persons involved in an accident can be very important to you.

You will agree how important it is, if you are the one injured. But you need to bear in mind that injuries to others can affect you in many other ways. Since we are talking about collecting insurance money, you should be aware that the more injuries there are in a single accident, the less likely you are to get as much as you might if there were only one injury - yours.

Earlier we talked about *Policy Limits*. The Policy Limit is the maximum amount the insurance company will pay for a certain type of claim under certain circumstances. The limit may be written on a *Single Limit* basis, which means that the insurance company will pay no more than a certain amount of money for all claims of all kinds in one accident. For example: If a policy has a single limit of $100,000, that is all the insurance company will have to pay out under any circumstance, unless they do something wrong, but we'll get to that later. If one person is seriously injured, that person could collect as much as the whole $100,000! But if ten people were injured, the most that all ten of them could get as a group would be $100,000.

I know it sounds like they would each get $10,000, but it doesn't work that way either. Each person might collect an amount of money different from all others based on the value of that person's particular claim.

Cutting Up The Pie

Although it is hard to imagine, just suppose that there were 50 people seriously injured, like in an airplane or bus crash. Suppose each of them has a claim which is worth a $100,000! The most each person could get in that case would be $10,000! Whoa!

But let's look at a simple car wreck where the owner of the car which caused the accident has a minimum split limit policy. If the law in your state provides for minimum policy limits of $20,000 per person for bodily injury, the policy limits would look like this: "20/40/15" or some similar combination. What that means is that each person injured can collect up to $20,000, BUT everyone injured in that one accident could only collect a combined total of $40,000. If only two people are injured, okay. But what if three are injured? Or four? Or more? Five people injured in the same accident could only collect a combined total of $40,000.

Well, it gets worse. What if one of the five was so seriously hurt that his claim was worth $100,000? He would probably collect $20,000, leaving a total of $20,000 for the remaining four injured people! If any of them were seriously injured or killed, you can see that the remaining twenty grand won't go very far. So the number of injuries and the severity of each of them can seriously and adversely affect your ability to collect insurance money even though you may have quite a lot coming to you.

Oh, the 15 in 20/40/15? That is for property damage. Woe be unto the owner of a thirty or forty-thousand-dollar car totaled or even seriously damaged in an accident with this guy. You're all right if the car you were driving at the time of the accident is an 18-year-old clunker, but if you were even driving a new compact car, you know that $15,000 won't go very far. Policy limits vary from state to state and from year to year. You may see very high limits and you will certainly see very low limits, but whatever the limits, it is very important for you to make note of all damages, especially injuries to people.

So look around. Ask questions. Who is hurt? How badly? Were they taken to a hospital in an ambulance? Was there any bleeding? Were there any obvious broken bones? While writing out your recollections of the accident, ask yourself if there was anyone limping or holding an arm or their head or any other part of their body. Was anyone lying down? Was anyone trapped inside a vehicle? And remember those who acted unhurt. Remember the ones who said they felt fine and were not hurt at all. Once some of them find out there is insurance money available, some imaginative injuries may come into existence. The "runners" have a lot to do with that, too. Each claim they develop will probably cut into the amount of insurance money you can collect.

Hunters . . .

The saddest feature of any accident, whether it be an automobile collision or a slip and fall on a wet floor or food poisoning, is that the unfortunate folks who really get hurt are often thrown together in most peoples' minds with the people who make up their aches and pains just to collect insurance money. As you can see, there is a great possibility of the people genuinely hurt in an accident getting less than they should because of undeserving *claimants* getting their hands into the *deep pockets* of the insurance companies. Hey! Two new terms!

"Claimants?" That is anyone who is making a claim against someone else. The term includes a person making a claim against his own insurance company, although insurance professionals usually call the latter: "Insureds." If you eavesdrop on adjusters talking, you will frequently, and I mean a LOT, hear them say these words. "The insured . . . blah, blah, blah." Or "The claimant . . . blah, blah, blah." When the adjuster says "insured," he means the person insured under a policy of insurance issued by the company for whom that adjuster works. When he says "claimant," he is talking about "the other guy." Usually, the person making a claim against the adjuster's "insured."

. . . *And Prey*

And deep pockets! The term *Deep Pockets* refers to a legal principle in some states called *Joint and Several Liability.* The deep pockets belong to the party who has the most money available to pay claims. That may mean an insurance company or it may mean a very wealthy person or even a private company such as a large corporation.

The principle of joint and several liability is based on the idea that if more than one person does something wrong which causes damage to another, all of them are responsible. Therefore all of them can be made to pay the damages. Then in a slight perversion, it was converted to mean that EACH one of them owes THE ENTIRE AMOUNT. To put it another way, if they all owe, they must all pay, and if one or more has no money with which to pay and some do, the fellows who have the money are forced to pay the full bill!

Let's see how this works. Let's say that two guys do something which is negligent and together makes up the proximate cause of a third person's injury. Let's further suppose that one of the two guys is 90% at fault and the other is 10% at fault. If the 90-percenter is broke, that is, has no money or property with which to pay the claim, the poor sap who was only 10% at fault can be made to pay THE WHOLE THING! If the 90-percenter has no insurance and the 10-percenter does, who do think is going to pay the claim? Why - the insurance company, of course!

I'm sure there are 9,462 lawyers out there who will probably say my analogy is faulty, but I really don't care. I think you get the point anyway. After all, collecting insurance money is BIG, BIG BUSINESS. This Deep Pockets thing is so big that many reforms are underway to change the system. I may have to rewrite this portion of the book in a future edition.

Down The Prim Rose Path

Have I mentioned "runners" often enough yet without explaining what I mean? It is appropriate to discuss them further in this chapter because they have much to do with the amount of "blood on the ground." A so-called "runner" is a person who works for a finder's fee. He is sort of like a bounty hunter except that he doesn't chase down criminals - he creates them! That may not be entirely fair since many runners start out "chasing ambulances." I'm not going to explain that one to you. I'm afraid you might burn my book if I did.

"Runners" are basically fellows who contact people injured in accidents of one kind or another and try to get them to sign up with a lawyer. You may have already been contacted by one yourself. If you already have a lawyer, that may be how you came to be represented in the first place. Runners offer all kinds of inducements to claimants in order to get them to become clients. Sometimes, it is merely the good neighborly advice that the person would be better off with an attorney, insurance adjusters being such liars and all. It may be the promise of a bigger pay off when the claim settles. But far too often it is the outright offer and/or payment of bribe money to get the client "signed up."

Obviously, the runner collects his money from a lawyer. Runners come in a variety of packages. Some dress as "investigators." Some pretend to be "paralegals" and some just out and out lie when they tell you that they themselves are in fact - lawyers. Believe it or not, some actually tell you that they work for attorneys and get paid for bringing in new clients. There are many stories, some pathetic, some ridiculous and some quite funny about runners and how they work and sometimes get caught in the act. Learn how to recognize them and if you spot one, know that what he is doing is at least unethical and at worst downright criminal - and stay away from them. If you need a lawyer, there are much better ways of finding one than going through a runner.

The runner generates claims, lawsuits, phoney injuries and fraud. That all costs you money. It causes your insurance rates to rise and may even reduce the amount of insurance money you are able to collect whether you are entitled to it or not.

Like Flies To Honey

Blood on the ground or anywhere for that matter except inside a human being is grotesquely alluring. It captures people's attention and excites them in a morbid fashion. The excitement ranges from nausea to gruesome obsession. The sights and sounds of an automobile accident draws the curious to its scene. A person falling down in a grocery store brings bystanders to immediate attention. They come to help, they come to look and sometimes they come to vicariously enjoy the carnage. But everyone who comes to the scene of an accident or is at the scene of an accident at the time it happens shares one thing in common. They are all *witnesses.*

Witnesses to an accident matter. They are very important. They can make the difference between collecting insurance money and **not** collecting insurance money. A witness can change an insurance company's denial of a claim into immediate settlement and payment. And there are countless cases where the discovery of a witness to the accident made it possible for the insurance company to avoid paying any money at all. It is therefore important for you to know about any possible witness to your accident.

You need to know if anyone witnessed the accident. You need to know what the witness is likely to say about the accident. And of special importance is the question of what the witness will say about you. Is the witness for you or against you? If the witness is for you, is the witness a friend or relative of yours? A friend, who happens to be a witness to your accident may not be as effective as you might think. The adjuster will discount the testimony of a friend or relative. It is probably fair to assume that your buddy or your girl friend might be somewhat biased in your favor and may not tell the truth, the whole truth and nothing but the truth. It makes a difference. On the other hand, if the witness is a friend or relative of "the other guy," he may try to hurt you by slanting his version of the accident in favor of his friend or relative. But, if you can show his relationship, whatever he has to say will have less effect.

However, a witness, whether biased or prejudiced or not, can hurt you. Witnesses, of course, can also help you a great deal. It all depends on what they say or what they are willing to say to the insurance adjuster. What the witness has to say or is willing to say depends to a large degree on what happens to the witness between the time of the accident and the time he gives his version of the accident to someone else. That may not sound like it makes sense. Shouldn't the witness just say what he saw? Isn't that all there is to it? No.

When we witness events in our lives, we don't consciously record how we will report those events later. We really don't have the time to do that while witnessing an event. Our minds are busily recording data in a flat, chronological pattern. That is, we just let the information enter through our senses and into our brains as it happens. Putting it in order and arranging it in a colorful, emotional or factual presentation is something we do later. Later is usually the first time someone asks us about it.

One of the most important functions of any investigator is to try to be the first to interview a witness. Without even realizing that we do it, when we ask people questions about the events in their lives, we actually influence how and what they are going to say. A skilled interrogator can change a hostile witness into a friendly witness. Even an unskilled person may have a profound effect of the witness' later versions of his story. It happens in the way the questions are asked. Questions can be asked in a positive way or a negative way. "Was the driver of the blue car drunk?" "How fast was the speeding car going?" "Did the Ford try to stop before it ran the red light?" Think about those questions. They are questions, but they are tainted. Whether the person who asked the questions knew or not, the questions are slanted toward getting a certain type of answer.

Well, try these on for size instead: "How fast were the cars going prior to the impact?" "Do you have any reason to believe that either of the drivers had been drinking alcoholic beverages prior to the accident?" "Which of the cars ran the red light?" "Did either driver try to slow down before the collision?" Etc. Etc. Etc. These questions seek answers. They are open questions which can be easily answered either way, but all too often, the first person to interview a witness is a partisan.

That is, he has an interest in the witness' story turning out a certain way. He can go a long way in seeing to it that the witnesses tells the kind of story he wants told instead of just telling what happened.

Ideally, a witness should be allowed to tell his story in his own way, but that rarely happens. It rarely happens because every witness concentrates on a very small part of the whole event. In telling his story, a witness will leave out very important details which for some reason or other have no interest to him. If the witness is allowed to just say what he wants, no one will ever know "the rest of the story." I have had witnesses say to me: "Your guy was going too fast!" "And that's all I got to say!" And, "He should have seen that little old lady and her family as they were slowly walking across the street in front of him!" No, no, I'm just kidding about the last part.

Foot In Mouth!

When I was a young adjuster, I was interviewing a man who witnessed a particularly distressing accident at a highway intersection. Both vehicles were traveling at a high rate of speed. One of them, a Chevrolet, blew through a stop sign at 60 miles an hour. That was my guy. The other vehicle was a 2-1/2 ton loaded water truck, going at least the same speed. But the truck had the right of way. In telling me his version of the accident, the witness, who had been following behind the water truck, told me that the front of the Chevrolet hit the side of the truck.

It is important to understand the position from which the witness saw the collision. He was not aware of the movement of the truck since it was going the same direction and speed in which the witness was traveling. He was aware most acutely of the great speed of the Chevrolet as it came out from the side road into the highway ahead. The physical evidence clearly showed that the front of the truck had smashed into and almost through the left side of the Chevrolet, killing and dismembering its driver on impact. It was not even an important point.

But the witness had told it wrong. I, in my zeal to get it "right," tried to repeat his answer back to give the witness an opportunity to verify his first statement or correct it if he wanted. Remember, I knew the actual facts. I was not guessing. I had already seen the vehicles. I had a picture of the front grille guard of the truck embedded in the side of the remains of the Chevrolet! So I tried to repeat his answer back to him. I said: "Now, you said that the front of the truck hit the side of the Chevrolet." I swear to you now, I did not intend to say it that way. I meant to say exactly what he had said to me, but for some weird reason, I reversed what he said to me and it was a huge mistake. The man, who was much larger than I am, pushed my small portable typewriter at me, stood up shaking his fists at me and ordered me out of the house while calling me choice, but forbidden, names. I tried in every way I could to apologize - explaining that I had simply made a mistake, but he was having none of that! He told me he could tell I was trying to make him change his story, and if I didn't get out of his house and off his property he would do things to me that I really didn't want him doing. So, I left. I apologized, but he did not even come close to believing me.

The ironic thing about it is that had I wanted to try to get him to change his story, I would have needed a much better ploy than that to get the job done. The story illustrates an important point. Witnesses see things from their own physical perspective and from their own personal point of view. The witness I spoke of above worked in a job related to the job of the water truck driver. He regarded the driver of the Chevrolet as an outsider, not one of them. He was not about to allow anything he said appear to help the driver of the Chevrolet in any way. And, as I said, it was not an important point. It didn't even matter! The man driving the Chevrolet clearly caused the accident and his own death.

But for me to even accidently suggest to the witness that he was wrong about his facts caused hard feelings which the man probably still talks about today. By the way, if you happen to be reading this, Mr. Anonymous Witness, YOU WERE WRONG! He has probably spent a lifetime telling people how he caught that lying adjuster trying to cheat one of his buddies out of some claim money. I'm sorry I said it wrong. I'm sorry the man got angry with me. I wish that I had handled it better, but I didn't. And it illustrates the problems and the importance of dealing carefully with witnesses and the need for you to accurately keep track of witnesses' names, addresses, phone numbers and what you understand that the witness is prepared to say about the accident.

Witnesses, runners and blood all around. Sometimes I think that is all accident investigation is about so far as insurance adjusters are concerned. For you, keep in mind that all of these factors can seriously affect the amount of insurance money you can successfully collect or whether you will get any at all. Wait a minute. We can't leave injuries without talking about yours.

6 I Feel Gooood! I Feel Baaaad!

You are sitting in your recliner watching as the commercials begin to interrupt your favorite program. That urge to be in the kitchen in front of the refrigerator or to be in the hall bathroom comes over you. You lean forward preparing to get up out of the chair, when suddenly an ice pick is driven into your lower back! The pain is sharp and searing! Your brain tells you that it is not really an ice pick, but the pain feels like it.

Someone calls your name. You turn to look in the direction of the person calling you and your head seems to be locked in position with a broad, burning sensation in your shoulder. The pain is so severe that you feel as though you cannot move! As you hold yourself stiff to avoid increasing the pain, it begins to spread over your shoulder and up into the base of your skull. You become frightened. You can't move!

Up until this moment you felt fine. What happened? It has been more than 24 hours since your car was rear-ended at a red light yesterday morning on your way to work. You were fine after the accident. You even told the police officer that there was no need for an ambulance. You were fine! Now, sitting in your chair at home, relaxed, watching television, you experience pain as you've never experienced before. What is going on?

Well, what may be, and probably is, going on is that your body is finally catching up to the events of yesterday morning. It is finally telling you: "YOU WERE INJURED YESTERDAY,

NUMB SKULL!" And you had better do something about it because it will get a lot worse before it gets better. The pain you feel may be the result of the abnormal stretching of muscles in your neck and back. Every doctor will have his own, as well as the standard medical profession, answer as to how and why this happens. You will know, if you don't know it already, that the pain occurs when a muscle experiences a spasm. That is, it tightens up like a knotted rope. In fact, if you find the muscle or group that is causing the pain, you will be able to feel a lump which feels as hard as a rock. That is muscle spasm and it is very painful!

The Cure

The suggested remedies range from rest to surgery. It is always a good idea to see your doctor as soon as possible after feeling the pain. He may prescribe a muscle relaxant drug. He may suggest massage and heat therapy. In extreme cases he may even suggest a cervical collar or soft neck brace to aid in taking normal strain off the muscles of your neck. He might even suggest stretching the muscle in some kind of traction device. If you see a Chiropractor, you can rest assured that he will at least suggest traction.

How much of this kind of treatment is necessary and how much really works is more than I can tell you. It turns out to be an individual thing. How healthy you were to begin with. The competence of your physician. Your relationship with your physician. How faithful you are about following the doctor's recommendations. And your attitude toward the injury and your recovery from it. I think the latter is probably the most important.

I had a druggist once who had the best remedy I have heard of yet. It worked, according to the doctor/pharmacist, on headaches as well as muscle aches and pains. He suggested, and by the way it was really a "he" in this case, that you should take two aspirins with a bottle of beer, lie down and relax. That's it. That's the whole treatment. Of course, it should be repeated as often as needed. My problem was that I don't like beer. I asked if Coca Cola would do. He advised me that it would not work since Coke was a stimulant and what I needed was something to relax me and my muscles.

See what I meant about attitude? If you're not willing to do what is necessary, the recovery will be slow, painful and long.

One of the biggest dangers in injuries of this type to muscles is the chance of the condition become chronic. Chronic means that the muscle once injured and not properly healed is more likely to be injured much more easily in the future. It can mean a life time of pain and discomfort from the same injury recurring over and over again. You need to take care of it. It may not matter a great deal as to which type of physician you seek for treatment, but I suggest seeing your family doctor, or if you have no family doctor, any physician who has treated you in the past who might have records of your medical history. A doctor, what I'm trying to say, who is already familiar with you - a doctor with whom you already have a relationship and maybe in whom you already have confidence.

Your relationship with the physician and your attitude will, I believe, have more to do with the success of your recovery than any other single thing. You will need to follow his directions, take the medication, do the exercises, get the therapy - whatever is prescribed until the damage has had a chance to repair itself. And please believe me when I say: "repair itself." Doctors do not heal you. You heal you. Well, really, your body heals itself, if you let it. But the doctor is your best guide. Listen to and act on his advice for your good health.

Feet Of Clay

Does it sound to you like I am promoting the interests of the doctors? Well, before you start to believe that, let me warn you that I am as critical of doctors in insurance claims as I am of lawyers. Many of us remember a time when the word of a doctor was second only to the word of God. We believed everything the doctor had to say. What a mistake that has become! Why do you think I make such a big deal out of going to a doctor you already know and trust? There are doctors practicing what they call medicine today who are not much better than prostitutes when it comes to what they will tell your lawyer for the right fee and for multiple referrals.

I read medical reports from doctors every day which sound like the pleadings in the lawyers' lawsuit. The doctors write reports as though they were standing in a ringside box seat at the time of the accident, saw everything that happened in great detail, inside and outside of the cars, AND know the law well enough to explain it IN THE MEDICAL REPORT! What's the deal here? I thought the doctor should tell me what kind of injury the person sustained and what he suggested about treatment and what he thought about the person's probable or likely recovery. Poor dumb me!

Many of these medical reports are produced on computers. Almost every word is the same except the patient's name and the date of the accident in report after report.. (Notice I said date of the accident, not date of the injury. Because that is what many of these doctors do.) The amount of treatment rendered and the total charges for these treatments have a mysterious way of being very much alike from patient to patient.

How High The Moon

You remember earlier we talked about policy limits? Well, there are various parts of an insurance policy which have different limits. For example, Personal Injury Protection, or PIP for short. This is a coverage in my state which provides for a form of *No Fault* protection. Now, we need to talk about some terms again. *No Fault* insurance is a form of insurance which will pay for your medical bills and sometimes even some of your lost wages if your injury results from an automobile accident. There are states which have made it the law of the state that everyone have No Fault insurance instead of the older liability form of policy.

Medical Payments Coverage is another form of No Fault protection which only pays for medical bills, not wages or any other kind of damages. PIP and Medical Payments always have a policy limit.

Typically, policies in our state have PIP limits of $2,500. There are other limits available and states differ on the amounts offered. But, when the policy limit on PIP is $2,500, treatment usually stops soon after the doctor's total charges reach that amount. It is laughable and pathetic to see how many doctor bills we receive from lawyers in the amount of approximately $2,700!

Insurance bought to protect a person's home is usually sold in policies known as *Homeowners* policies. These policies carry Medical Payments Coverage and often have limits of $5,000, although they can have other limits. Frequently in claims arising out of injuries sustained around someone's house, the medical treatment is most often successful soon after the bills exceed - take a guess - $5,000! If these sorts of things happened only occasionally, few if any of us would think much about it. But, ask any adjuster, you will learn that it happens far too many times for it to be just coincidental.

Are some doctors "in bed" with some lawyers? If you don't believe it, perhaps you might be interested in buying the bridge over the Houston Ship Channel? I can get it for you, cheap! I guess the next question is: "Do you need a doctor like this?" NO! NO! NO! There should only be one reason for seeing a doctor. There is only one legitimate reason. That reason is to treat a real injury and to recover from the injury as early and successfully as possible. Going to a doctor just to run up some phoney medical expenses in order to build up a fraudulent insurance claim is criminal! Part of my job and the job of every hard working adjuster is to try to catch you and your lawyer and your doctor if that is what you are doing!

But, if you are injured - if you think you are injured - go see a doctor. Get treatment and get well! During the process keep track of all your expenses in connection with the treatment. Because the amount of your medical bills will have an important effect on the amount of insurance money you can collect. Perhaps, you will begin to see why a lawyer would want to send his clients to a particularly friendly, useful and greedy doctor.

Multiplication Tables

There is a "rule" in the insurance claim business called the *Three Times Specials* rule. You won't find it in the law books. You won't find it in the medical books. Most insurance company people will deny that it even exists. Many lawyers will tell you that you have the name wrong. "It is not the three-times special rule," they will say. "It is the *four point three* times rule." Let's try to clear this up.

To begin with, *Special Damages* are amounts of money included in a judgment of a lawsuit based on specific amounts which can be proved by bills, receipts and other hard copy evidence of expenses incurred <u>because of</u> the injury complained of in the lawsuit. Other types of damages include *General* damages and *Exemplary* or punitive damages. General damages include such items as *Pain and Suffering*, *Mental Anguish* and *Loss of Consortium.* In other words, items of damage which must be guessed at or estimated in the opinion of a judge or a jury. Punitive damages are what you might think they are. It is the legal system's way of spanking the wrongdoer in an effort to teach him not to do it again. It doesn't work and I'll tell you why later.

But, back to the three-times-special rule. When the lawyer starts to ring the bell on his cash register, he uses such "rules" to estimate how much money he can ask the insurance company to pay his client. If the medical bills total $2,500, the lawyer multiplies $2,500 by three to arrive at a starting point for his evaluation. In this way he says the claim is worth $7,500. Lawyers and adjusters often disagree (News flash!), they disagree as to what to multiply three by. The lawyers will sometimes include lost wages in the total with the medical bills and then multiply by three. So if the medical bills are $2,500 and the claimant lost three weeks' work at $500 per week, he comes up with a total of $4,000. He multiplies this figure by three and gets $12,000 and joyfully calls the insurance company to collect.

I have had lawyers correct me and tell me that the rule is really the *four point something* times the damages rule. Read: 4.2 times. Okay, $4,000 times 4.2 equals (Wow!) $16,800! The lawyer's share: at least $5,544! Good arithmetic, I'd say. But, 4.2, or anything other than three times, is pure mythology. There is a reason. The three-times rule grew out of the need for fairness in splitting the insurance proceeds between the claimant, his lawyer and his doctor. So, if the insurance settlement is $7,500, remember the lawyer's contract, he gets one-third, or $2,500. Well, shouldn't the claimant get as much as the lawyer? And what about the doctor? He made this all possible. If you want to be fair, give him $2,500 as well.

You can see that if the lawyer gets a third, he must collect enough money to pay the doctor and still give his client at least as much money in the original split as the lawyer gets himself. Of course, as you may learn, the expenses come out of your third, not the lawyer's. In order to achieve this fine balance, you need only to start out with the doctor's share, multiply it by three and VOILA! a settlement everyone can live with - even the insurance companies, for they understand better than most exactly how the system works.

Why not 4.3 times the special damages? Well, just because! I mean, the "rule" is three times, and that's that. Look at it this way, if the doctor gets $1,000, the lawyer and the claimant each want $1,000 as well. If each of three people get $1,000, then each gets a one-third share. So, three times the medical. Therefore, the rule is three times whatever to get to the value of the claim.

There is a lot more to evaluating claims that has been discussed here as you will see. But for now it is enough for you to know how important medical bills are to determining just how much insurance money you can collect. I should clear something up. So far, I've made it sound like the doctor himself gets one-third of the insurance claim settlement. Although that may be true in some cases, you need to remember that hospital bills, ambulance bills, the cost of prescription medicines, crutches, splints and therapy are all included in special damages. In fact, the doctor may get only a very small portion when compared to the entire insurance settlement. Sorry, Docs, I didn't mean to make you sound that bad.

The Proof Is In The Papers

Your injury is important. It is important to your health. It is important to your comfort or the lack of it. It is important to your insurance claim. Keep good records. Save all of your receipts and bills. Keep canceled checks and credit charge slips. Don't throw away that sack your prescription medicine came in, save it along with the receipt. It will become useful when you begin evaluating your claim and entering negotiations with the adjuster. And you will have to have it to present to the adjuster to prove your claim and collect the amount of insurance money you deserve.

Crutches, Collars And Showing Off

Finally in connection with your injuries, if the doctor prescribes a neck collar, or if your arm is supposed to in a sling, or you need to use crutches for a while to help the healing process, don't be embarrassed by it. Wear the collar. Place your arm in the sling and walk on the crutches if you need to. But DON'T, whatever you do, think for one moment that using these devices are going to in any way influence your adjuster into thinking your claim is worth more money than it is. The trick of putting the collar on in your car just before going into the adjuster's office is old and trite.

I can't count the number of times I have knocked on a claimant's door and, after identifying myself though the door, had to stand waiting an unreasonably long time while the claimant rushed to the bedroom and hurriedly placed the collar around his neck before admitting me to his home. If you need the collar, wear it as long as you need to, but quit when the medical reason for wearing the collar no longer exists. The adjuster will know, and his opinion of you and your claim will be shaped in part by what he thinks of your honesty and integrity.

If you are hurt, get treatment and get well. Make an appropriate claim and deal with the adjuster honestly. Do not fabricate an injury in order to collect insurance money - they call that fraud and it is a crime. One which can send you straight to jail! The adjuster will be sympathetic. He is, after all, human too. He is not looking for a way to get out of paying you insurance money. He is only trying to gather enough information to determine if you are entitled to money in the first place and, if so, to calculate how much you have coming. Keep in mind that it is not his money. It belongs to the insurance company and they got it from you and me to begin with. We paid it to the insurance company so that the insurance company would have money to pay us back when and if we need and deserve it.

By the way, guess where the money comes from to pay *punitive* damages. It comes from the insurance company. That's right, the money you and I pay into the insurance company so there will be money there when we need it. That same money is used for the punishment to a wrongdoer! You will recall I said that it doesn't work? Well, that's why. Punitive damages reward an injured person and his attorney beyond what the injured person is entitled to collect. The courts tell us that the purpose is to punish the wrongdoer. But who gets punished? The money comes from the insurance company and the insurance company gets all of its money from you! So you are being punished for something someother jerk did wrong! Each time you pay insurance premiums, you may be throwing in a little something as a penalty for something you had nothing to do with.

As I said, it doesn't work and anyway, you won't be concerned with it. In order to even discuss punitive damages, lawyers must be involved. They speak that language. You and your insurance adjuster won't. Remember, you're collecting insurance money without a lawyer. And it's important for you to realize, that stuff you see in newspapers or hear on television about huge puntive damage settlements is in the twilight zone as far as you are concerned. Stick to what really matters in your settlement.

7 My Merry Oldsmobile Ain't So Merry Anymore.

Whether the love of your life is a 1964 Chevrolet Tudor Super Sport, a 1977 Buick Park Avenue or a brand new Lincoln Town Car right off of the show room floor, you will have feelings for the car you drive which sometimes may seem unrealistic. After all, it is only a machine. Right? Well, it may just be a machine, but automobiles have become more than mere forms of transportation. This is especially true in the United States where Americans have had a love affair going with cars since Henry Ford developed a means of mass producing them. And at no time are a person's feelings about and attitude toward a car as evident as it is following an accident in which that car has been injured...hurt...no, I mean damaged.

Car owners, even though injured themselves will, at times, act more concerned and perhaps get more upset and angry over their cars being damaged than they get over their own personal bodily injuries. It's true! Possession of a car becomes enormously important to us long before we are either old enough or physically big enough to actually drive one. With the coming of 'teen' age, it sometimes becomes an obsession with us. We must have a car. Our lives depend upon having a car. We will become social outcasts without a car. We <u>must</u> have WHEELS! And once we have them, nothing in life is ever the same again.

There occurs in life a dramatic change when a person becomes the owner of an automobile. The remnant of control which our parents once wielded over us is now for the most part vanished. Only the best behaved and noblest of us are able to resist the temptation to set our own agendas and time schedules once in possession of an automobile. We simply turn into completely autonomous beings when we feel those keys in our hands! Although we may have great intentions in the beginning - you know: how we are going to be careful, not drink when we drive, be home on time, not let an unlicensed driver operate the car? And, I promise . . . , I promise . . . , I promise . . . ? Those good intentions are soon forgotten and we become **independent**.

It is easy to see how important a car can become when you consider the impact a car can have on a person's independence. The feelings are far deeper and more wide ranging than just a vehicle to be used to get from here to there. It is emotionally as much a part of us as our families. Sometimes, as dear to us as our sisters and brothers, mothers and fathers, and sometimes more important than our relationships with our relatives and friends. A car can mean **freedom!**

So if anything happens to our car, we get emotionally involved very quickly. We can't get to work. We can't go out with friends. We can't do our shopping. Modern life and the American love affair with the automobile has so completely changed the way we live and our attitudes toward life that to be without a car is much like being stranded on a desert island. If you only own one car, its absence can be devastating and even a very minor collision of the car with another object can render it useless.

If the damage resulting from the collision involves the lights, the windows, the doors, the wheels, the steering or any of assorted other systems the car cannot be driven either legally, safely or mechanically. Often, even though the car looks as though it has very little or no damage at all, it still cannot be driven, making a very frustrating situation for you. When that happens, you need a substitute vehicle.

"*Wheels While Your Car Heals*"

The slogan of a well known car rental company reflects in a cute way the relationship of rental cars and automobile accident. While your car is sick or broken, you need alternate transportation, hence, "Wheels While Your Car Heals." Or to put it another way, some way to get around, to get to work, to go shopping or to go out with friends until your car can be repaired or replaced and put back into service. You might not think that the subject of a rental car would come up first, but it nearly always does. Substitute transportation nearly always takes precedence over the amount of damage to your wrecked car or how to go about repairing or replacing it.

Believe it or not, few people know what to do about rental cars. For most people, the only connection they have ever had with the car rental business is through watching commercials on television promoting one car rental company over another. One company calls itself, "Number One" in the industry, while another claims to be second but is employee owned and working hard to overtake "Number One." And so forth. These top line car rental companies charge top line prices. The rental rates range from about thirty dollars a day to close to one hundred dollars a day. If you call one of these companies, you will be paying out more for the rent car than you can possibly collect from an insurance company.

Earlier, we talked about policy limits. In addition to the formal policy limits in insurance policies, there are also various other kinds of limitations. One of them involves rental cars directly. If your policy has coverage for damage to your automobile called *Comprehensive* or *Other Than Collision*, it will probably also include *Theft Rental Reimbursement.* The coverage usually has a time deductible as well as daily and monthly limits as to the amount of money the policy will pay. For example, most policies will not begin paying theft rental reimbursement until 48 hours after the theft occurs. This is called a time deductible. It provides for a period of time following the loss during which you will have to pay for the rent car yourself. However . . .

(Now listen closely - If you ask the right question, the rent car company may waive the first two days rental for you in order to get you to rent a car from them instead of some other car rental company.)

After the 48 hour period passes, the insurance coverage kicks in but only for a set amount each day, usually about 20 dollars, although the amount varies from state to state. This means that when you rent a substitute car, it is important to make sure the car rental company intends to charge you no more than the daily limit since that amount is all the insurance company will pay. Furthermore, most policies provide that you can only collect rental reimbursement for a period of 30 days. Even though it is the 30-day period which is important, it may be stated as a maximum amount of money which is calculated by multiplying the daily rate times 30 days. If the daily maximum is $20 then the maximum limit of the policy for any one theft is $600 which of course is $20 times 30 days.

Another coverage offered by insurance companies is *Collision Rental Reimbursement.* This must be purchased as an extra feature and you will be charged an additional premium for the coverage. It differs from theft rental reimbursement in three major ways. First, you get the coverage automatically with theft coverage, but not with collision coverage. Secondly, theft rental reimbursement costs you nothing extra but collision rental reimbursement does. And thirdly, in order to qualify for theft rental, you need only prove that your car was stolen and has been missing for 48 hours or more. Eligibility for collision rental reimbursement depends on your car being withdrawn from use because of its physical breakdown and/or need for repair.

The repairs can be made necessary by a car wreck or by the engine breaking down for some mechanical reason. The only requirement, in addition to having the coverage, is that the car actually be damaged or broken down in such a way that it must be placed in a repair shop to get it back to running again. Your insurance company will then pay for the cost of renting a car while your car is being repaired. Those are the two ways you can collect insurance money from your own insurance company for car rental. But there is another and in many ways much more important situation in which you can collect insurance money for a rent car, when you collect insurance money from someone else's insurance company.

"Loss Of Use"

An insurance policy bought to protect one person from claims made against them by someone else is called a *Liability Policy.* One of the two coverages most often purchased is called *Property Damage Liability.* It covers the policyholder's obligation to another person as a result of damaging that other person's property - most often that other person's car. It can, however, be any kind of property: a fence, a garage, a bicycle, a boat. When your property is damaged, your loss includes the cost of repairing or replacing the property. It includes any decrease in value the property may suffer, as a result of the damage, and it includes your loss of use - the loss you sustain by not being able to use the property simply because it is has been damaged.

In the case of an automobile, loss of use describes the loss you suffer by not being able to drive the car, not being able to use it to get to work, to go shopping and so on. Your loss of the property's utilitarian value for the time it is out of service due to the damage can be measured in dollars and cents and it adds up to money you can collect from an insurance company. Now, although technically there is no limit, either daily or otherwise, as to how much someone might owe you for loss of use, there are guidelines which must be followed.

To begin with, the courts impose a limit by requiring that the measure of damage be reasonable. If you own a small inexpensive compact car, you will not be entitled to collect rental money to drive a large, high-dollar luxury car while your car is being repaired. If your car is considered to be a total loss as a result of the damage, you will find it difficult to collect loss of use or car rental money for more than a few days. Most insurance companies will agree to pay you for about a week of car rental until the damage can be appraised and a determination made showing the car to be a total loss.

But once the decision has been made to "total" the car, the loss of use is apt to be cut off. Think about it. If your car is totaled and the insurance company is willing to pay you the value of the car, should you have the right to demand more from the insurance company than the value of the car? Well, of course folks argue about that all the time and there are some variables. For example, you must have a reasonable amount of time to replace your car. But reasonable is for the courts to decide and you don't want to get involved in the courts if you don't have to. Why? I was afraid you wouldn't ask. Why? Because if the claim gets to a court, it has to go to a lawyer first, and I think we have already decided that you can collect more money for yourself without one.

The alternative is to work out the car rental portion of the loss with your insurance adjuster. To do this you need to know his rules. What do you think the first rule any insurance adjuster is going to think about in regard to rent cars? Give up? The adjuster will automatically, almost by reflex think, "The limit on rent cars is $20 per day." In addition to that, the adjuster will be able to refer you to dozens of car rental companies who will, in fact, rent a car to you for $20 day including any sales tax which might be imposed in the area where you live. Don't expect to get a limousine or a Mercedes for $20 a day, but you can get good, reliable transportation for that amount of money. After all, you're not going to be in the car very long. Repairs usually take from a day or two to about three weeks. Any longer than that, and someone needs to look into the possibility of a total loss. There can be reasons for the car to be tied up longer than that, but no insurance company should be required to pay extended car rental fees because the body shop lets your car sit in their shop collecting dust while they work on someone else's car.

For many years, most insurance companies would pay for the cost of renting a substitute car by the so-called *direct bill* method, which means the car rental company would allow you to use the rental car and send their bill directly to the insurance company for payment. You would be out nothing. All companies still use *direct bill* for theft rental and collision rental reimbursement, but few will allow it in connection with liability claims. The direct bill arrangement is so easily and often abused. Claimants will sometimes get a rental car and just keep it for many weeks and even months beyond a reasonable time. If the adjuster threatens to cut off the rental, the claimant may call the adjuster's "bluff" and threaten to hire a lawyer if the rent car is taken away.

The whole idea behind direct billing of rental cars was to accommodate claimants - to let them know the insurance company wanted to work with them - in order to avoid lawyer involvement. If the claimant uses the threat of a lawyer to influence the negotiations, most adjusters will feel that dealing with a lawyer would be easier than dealing with the claimant under the constant threat of hiring a lawyer. So, now, in most cases, you must pay for the rent car yourself and collect from the insurance company later. A method referred to as the *reimbursement* method.

Remember, to get the maximum recovery when collecting insurance money, it is important to get along with the adjuster. Work something out with him on the rent car. Be reasonable, but make your needs clear to the adjuster. If you have a special situation, carefully explain it. If your damaged vehicle is a van or pickup truck which is used for special purposes which an ordinary passenger car cannot fulfill, you will be entitled to rent a similar vehicle. The special insurance rates for rental cars applies only to passenger cars. All other types of vehicles will cost more money and those costs can be passed along to the insurance company as a part of your claim.

Specifically, if your car is damaged and cannot be driven, you are entitled to collect a reasonable sum of money to cover the cost of renting a substitute vehicle for the time it takes to repair or replace your damaged vehicle. Remember, we are talking about liability claims now. The daily rate will normally be the same as the maximum set in automobile insurance policies for thefts, even though the rule does not actually apply to liability claims.

The time it takes to repair your vehicle can be estimated by the person who inspects the damage and writes a *repair estimate*. That person may be an adjuster or it may be an appraiser. Either way, the time it will take to repair the damage will be calculated in one of many different ways. The time I refer to here is the number of days it will take to get your car finished and back in service. A good rule of thumb for you to follow is to check the total number of labor hours shown on the estimate. Divide this number by six. The result is the number of days it will take to repair the car. If that number is greater than five, you should add two extras days for the weekend. If a holiday occurs, add an extra day or days for that. When you get through adding all the extra days, throw in one more day for good measure and tell the adjuster to pay you for that number of days for your loss of use claim.

Say your estimate shows 38 labor hours including repair time and paint time. Divide 38 by six. The result is 6.3333333 days. Well, round that up to seven days. Since the total is more than five, add two for the week end. Now you have nine days. Suppose that the 4th of July is on Wednesday of the week the repairs are to be done. Add a day for that. You now have ten days. Throw in one extra day for good measure and you have a total of eleven days of car rental to collect. Now I will tell you a little secret. Ask the adjuster for three weeks of car rental. Why? Each week is measured by five working days. Eleven days is one day more than two weeks, so ask for three. The adjuster may negotiate you back to something less than 21 days, but make the best deal you can.

If your car is a total loss, you will probably get a rent car for seven to ten days during the time it takes to assign the claim to an adjuster or appraiser and get the inspection made and the estimate completed. If you have a case of *clear liability*, which means the facts of the accident are such that few would dare argue about whether you will be able to collect or not, you will be entitled to payment for loss of use until you can replace your damaged vehicle. But you can't dilly-dally around. You must get busy, find a suitable car and buy it! That may mean raising the money or getting new financing, but the courts impose on you a duty to *mitigate your damages.* Simply put, that means you should try to keep your damages as low as reasonably possible.

Usually this should present no problem for if it is a case of clear liability, the insurance company is required to pay your property damage claim promptly once liability has been established. Don't always expect the insurance company to pay for a rent car up to the day you actually get the settlement money in your hands because they don't have to do that. Most adjusters will, however, make every effort to get the money to you as quickly as possible. In return, they expect you to cooperate with them and get your car repaired or replaced as quickly as you can.

If your car is financed, that is, if you owe money to a bank or finance company for your car, you will probably be able to buy a replacement vehicle on a *substitution of collateral* basis. You notify the *lienholder* (the people you owe the money to on your car), that the car has been totaled in an accident. You tell them that you want to buy a replacement vehicle and substitute it as the collateral on your loan for the car which has been wrecked. It's just that simple. Few lienholders will turn you down since it is in their best interest to have good collateral on the loan. When their collateral has been wrecked and is sitting in a junk yard somewhere and there is an argument going on as to who is going to pay for the car, the lienholder's position is not a good one. They will welcome fresh collateral.

One final note on rent cars. Almost all rental companies will deliver the rental car to you and pick it up when you are through with it. If they don't, find another company to rent from. When you get ready to return the car, give the rental company at least one day's notice to allow proper scheduling of the pick up. Oh, and by the way, you may be required to put up a deposit. Usually this is done with a credit card. If you have no credit card you will be asked for a cash deposit. The insurance company will not pay it for you. If you have no credit card or cash, ask the adjuster to advance pay the loss of use claim. They don't have to do it. Remember what I said, it is important to get along with the adjuster to get what you want. If you start a fight, you will surely wind up having a lawyer collect the money for you and sharing it with you.

8 Fender Benders, Dings And Hammering Out The Damage.

The rental company just dropped off your substitute car and you begin to think about what to do about your damaged car. Where is it? What kind of condition is it in? Can it be repaired? How much will the repairs cost? Where will you get it repaired? (Can you get them to repair that old damage on the other side of the car?) ***Can you get the body shop to cover your deductible?***

First, you probably already know where the car is. If not, get a copy of the police report. If one was made, it will show you where the car was taken. Don't wait for an appraiser to get in touch with you. Call the agent, the adjuster, the insurance company - anyone you can - to find out who the appraiser is. Once you identify the appraiser, call him. Find out how soon your car will be inspected. Be reasonable, but don't let anyone stall you.

If the car is in your possession, make it available to the appraiser whenever it is needed. Go to some effort on your own to help make the arrangements and get the damage appraised as soon as possible. If your car is driveable, offer to drive it to the appraiser's office for inspection. Some companies will actually pay for the damage to the car on the spot if you take it to them for the estimate to be made. If you wind up in a hospital following the accident, don't worry about the car unless you feel up to dealing with it from your hospital bed. Let it sit. It is the adjuster's responsibility to begin an investigation promptly and that includes estimating the cost of repair or damage to your vehicle.

Once the car has been inspected, you should expect to get a copy of the repair estimate within 24 hours. If you don't, call the appraiser or the adjuster to find out why. Whether written by hand or on a computer, there is no excuse for the written estimate not to be completed by the day following the inspection. If something unusual causes a delay, get a complete explanation. Be patient, but not for long. If you suspect that someone is delaying unreasonably, ask to speak to a supervisor. Supervisors do not like getting calls from claimants or insureds and adjusters and appraisers do not like for you to call their supervisors. Although this can be a useful tool, DO NOT ABUSE IT. Use it only if you are convinced your claim is not being handled properly.

I said within 24 hours and I meant it. With FAX machines and overnight mail available, you should not have to wait long to get the estimate in your hands. I suggest strongly that you get a copy for yourself. Don't rely on your body shop to review the estimate, check it yourself even though it may look like a foreign language to you the first time you see it. A proper repair estimate can be read by any one.

The estimate will contain a list of parts. It will contain a list of operations to be performed on those parts. It will list the number of labor hours necessary to perform the listed operations. It will show the price of each part and show whether the part called for on the estimate is to be a new part or not. It will list the time required for painting parts which are repaired or replaced and the cost of the paint and materials necessary to complete the job. It may show items of work which are to be sub-let to another repair facility and it may show sales tax if applicable in your area. It should show the rates at which the labor is charged. The cost of body shop repair, painting and mechanical repairs may differ in their rates.

Repairs, Parts and Putty.

More arguments develop over the kind of part to use and whether a part can be repaired than possibly any other issue and there are many to argue over. Whether a part can be repaired or not depends upon how badly it is damaged. I'm not joking! I know you knew that, but how do you find out "how badly damaged" it is? Two things, first, can it be repaired? Although a judgment call, almost anyone can look at a part and know when it cannot be repaired. I mean if a fender or hood is simply crumpled up into a wad, my seven year old grandson could tell that it cannot be repaired! On the other hand, damage ranging from minor scratches to severe, but repairable damage must be estimated by professionals. At least two will be involved in any decision about your car - an appraiser and a body shop person. When the two of them agree that a part can be repaired, it can be repaired. When the two of them agree that the part cannot be repaired, no problemo. BUT, if they disagree as to whether a part can be repaired or not, tell them to repair it if they can, but if they can't you will insist on replacement without extra payment for the wasted time and the attempted repairs. In such cases, the appraiser will probably give in and agree to include replacement of the part in the estimate.

"You're not gonna put any old used parts on MY car!" Why not? The damaged part was an "old used part" before the accident. Insurance policies never refer to parts as used. The policy uses language like this, "a part of like kind and quality," often referred to as "LKQ" parts. It may be a used part, one taken from another car more seriously damaged than your own. Or it may be a so-called *after market part,* which means that someone other than your car's original manufacturer fabricated the part. Some are good, some not so good. Your body shop will let you know if the after-market part is one not-so-good. The important thing to know is there is nothing wrong with used parts or after market parts. It is far more important to know that the shop doing the repairs is experienced and skilled in repairing automobiles damaged in accidents.

LKQ parts help keep the cost of repairs down and in some cases they represent the only source for a replacement part for your car. Furthermore, new parts are not all they are cracked up to be. Often when a part does not easily fit onto a car during the manufacturing process, rather than slow the assembly line down, the part may be discarded in favor of another part to keep the line moving. Those parts removed from the line are not thrown away. They may be shipped to your local body shop to be put on your car as a replacement part. The thinking is that although the factory didn't have time to make the part fit, the body shop will. And besides, why is a new part better than an old one? If your car was built four years ago and there have been any production changes during that time, there will have been no new parts like that one produced. A part in stock may be four years old even though it has never been on a car.

If the estimate calls for used or after market parts, don't argue about it. You should be concentrating on the total amount of money you will collect, not quibbling over the age or source of a part. But if a dispute does develop, never pass up an opportunity to use it in your negotiations by reminding the adjuster that if what the insurance company is suggesting doesn't work out it will cost them more money to correct it later on.

The decision to repair a part or to replace it should be an easy one. If not, the appraiser should come down on the side of replacement, but if the estimate calls for repair, there are some things to consider which might make you feel better about it. A much bandied-about expression which is rapidly becoming trite due to its overuse is nevertheless a very good rule to follow. ***If it ain't broke, don't fix it!*** And if a part can be repaired, in most cases you are much better off repairing the old part than cutting the car apart in order to replace the part. Cars used to be bolted together for the most part. To replace something, a mechanic would loosen the bolts, disassemble the car, put it back together and bolt everything back into place. Almost no cars are assembled that way today. Unitized bodies, the use of fiberglass and welding parts together are now the hallmark of automobile manufacturing. To take many parts off of a car it is necessary to **cut the part out.**

When something is cut open, it can never be put back together exactly the same way again. Oh, they can make the car look fine, but why ask for trouble? Many parts, such as fenders, quarter panels, roof panels, floor pans and other parts can be more easily repaired while still on the car than they can be replaced. It is not even always true that the amount of the estimate would be higher from replacement as compared to repairs. The rule to follow is to do the best kind of repair which is called for in view of the specific damage sustained by your car. Repair the car as soon as possible, have the repairs done as well as possible, get the car back into service, turn in your rent car, if you have one, and get on with the business of collecting insurance money!

Will the cost of automobile repairs help your claim any from the stand point of how much money you can collect? The answer is no. Cars with damage as low as $147.50 have carried injured people whose claims totaled in the thousands of dollars. Although the amount of damage, or better stated, the extent of damage is often used as an indicator as to the possibility and severity of injuries to the car's occupants, it is certainly not conclusive. That is why it is pointless to waste time and energy arguing about how to repair the car and exactly how high the estimate is in dollars and cents. Just get it fixed and get on with more important things. And what about body putty?

BONDO! If you think for one minute that you can get a modern automobile repaired without using some kind of plastic body panel filler material, give it another thought. The reality is that body putty or bondo as it is often called is universally used to repair cars. In many cases the car simply could not be repaired economically without the use of such material. If it is applied correctly, the car will look fine and you will never know the filler is there. If an amateur applies it, or if an incompetent repairman uses body putty instead of *roughing out* the large dents and malformations of metal parts, you could have problems. But, since you are the person who selects the repairing facility, that is your responsibility. Make sure the body shop is qualified to do the work. And don't let your brother-in-law do it for you cheap!

Lookin' For A Place To Go.

There are ways to check up on a shop where you are thinking about having work done. You should begin by visiting the shop to see what it looks like. Ask yourself questions about the shop as you visit. Is the shop well equipped? You don't have to know what the tools and equipment are for, just look around to see what they have. The shop should look "lived in," That is, there should be on-going jobs or at least evidence showing work having recently been done. Don't worry about whether the shop looks "messy" or not. That is a judgment which you may not be qualified to make. Shops get dirty. But, on the other hand, if the shop is so cluttered with old parts, junk and odd collections of strange looking objects all covered with a heavy coating of dust, beware. If it is difficult to even walk through the shop, you will be seeing signs of neglect and laziness.

Sittin' an' a'thinkin'

Does the body shop have a waiting room? Many do not, but if it does, the waiting room does not necessarily have to look like the waiting room of your lawyer or your doctor, but it should have some chairs, a table or two, good lighting, something to read and it should be *relatively* quiet. Bear in mind that you are at a body shop where metal is being hammered and electric tools are being operated, so there will be some noise.

There should be some reading material handy even if it is old car magazines in which you have no interest. It may be important to note, however, that the more interest the people who operate your body shop have in automobiles, the more likely it is they are to know what they are doing. The air in the waiting room should be maintained at a comfortable temperature. It doesn't have to be perfect, just not too hot in the summer and not too cold in the winter. After all, you are not going to sit there the entire time your car is in the shop!

Takin' Care'a Bizness

The office, like the waiting room , is not going to be sterile. Conditions will vary from being somewhat dirty and cluttered to being clean, neat, orderly and efficient. But it should be large enough for the people who work there to work and still leave room for you. If you can't even get into the office, or even find the office, you may want to look for another shop to do the repairs. The office should be staffed by someone. If it is not, don't expect to be able to call on the telephone to check on your car because there won't be anyone there to answer the telephone. While you are in the office look at the walls. Check to see if they are members of the local Chamber of Commerce or any other professional or trade organizations.

In short, look the place over well. Are the employees of the shop dressed in uniforms? In fact are they dressed at all? When your inspection of the body shop reveals men stripped to the waist while working or if the manager of the shop is dressed in tank top, shorts and thongs, leave and go somewhere else. Make sure the entire place has a professional look about it. The people operating the shop should look like they care about you and your opinions. Otherwise, you don't need them. There are many shops who will.

Check to see if the repairmen are I-CAR certified technicians. Ask if the shop gives warranties on its work. The guarantee should be for a year or certainly no less than six months. Make sure the warranty is in writing. You will usually find it printed on the repair estimate. And while you're looking around ask to see a car which they have already repaired and is ready for delivery to its owner. This will give you the opportunity to check the quality of the shop's work first hand.

If it looks like a place where you want your car to be repaired, then by all means go ahead and do business with them. However, if it looks like a place you would never want to take your car to, much less to go yourself, skip it and look for another shop. If the shop meets with your approval, then go on to other means to check it out. Talk to customers.

Yes, just as in any other business, former customers of the shop can tell you much about their experience with the shop. And most will willingly let you know if they are unhappy with the results. Surprisingly, the people who had a pleasant repair experience and are happy with the results will usually talk your arm off about how good the shop is. So far so good, but how do you find old customers? Just ask the shop for references. Now, while it is true that the shop could give you the names and telephone numbers of "plants", selected friends who will say anything the shop owner asks them to say, you will be able to tell rather quickly if they are telling you the truth.

One good way to locate a body shop is to ask your friends to see if any of them have had a recent experience with a body shop. If so, ask them to tell you about the shop and then check it out as discussed above. Call the Better Business Bureau to find out if any complaints have been reported against the shop. Beware of shops where there appears to be a number of men sitting around doing nothing but loafing or "hanging out." If they are employees, business may be off because they are not any good at what they do. If they are not employees, the shop may be a hang out for derelicts, drunks and other assorted ner'-do-wells.

As I said earlier, you are responsible for selecting the shop which repairs your car. If you make a bad choice and the shop screws up the job of repairing your car, you will have no recourse against the insurance company. Delays, poor workmanship or lousy quality parts are matters you must take up with the body shop management. If the shop fails to deliver the car on time, you have no right to expect the insurance company to pay for the extra days of car rental. If the shop is at fault, make the shop supply you with a substitute vehicle or demand that they pay the extra car rental until the repairs can be completed. And stay on the shop manager's back until the job is finished. Don't let them push your car aside while they do other work.

If your car is still driveable, ask the shop which you select to do the repairs to order the parts right away. Don't leave your car with them to start work on it until they can assure you that the parts have already arrived and repairs can begin immediately and be completed right away. There is simply no sense in leaving a driveable car in a body shop to sit collecting dust while waiting for the parts to arrive from Taiwan. So to sum it up: be careful, ask questions, look around and satisfy yourself as to the selection of a repair facility before you sign anything authorizing repairs. You should know that you are the only one who can authorize repairs to a car which you own. No one else can do it. Not the adjuster, not the appraiser and not your mother-in-law. You must do it yourself.

But be careful!

Oh. And the deductible? Well, don't make a big deal out of it too early. In fact don't mention it all when you first begin talking with the body shop. However, when you get down to making a deal with the shop to repair your car don't hesitate to ask if they can help you with your deductible. Many shops will try to find out how much the deductible is before writing the repair estimate. No matter what they tell you, body shop appraisers routinely add in enough money to take care of contingencies such as your deductible and repairing old damage as well as extra money for themselves. Although it may not be ethical and adjusters will try to catch you at it, most shops will cover the policyholder's deductible in order to get the repair job into their shop. Consider it a finder's fee.

9 Oh, How I Hate To Get Up In The Morning!

Getting up in the morning is especially difficult if the morning is the day after your automobile accident. It is even more difficult if you were injured in the accident and are now suffering the pain and discomfort associated with those injuries. It is even difficult if you are on medication such as pain relievers, muscle relaxants or tranquilizers. And if you can't get up or don't feel like getting up, you can't go to work. This can result in the most severe financial hardship you face as a result of being injured in an accident. And this may be one of the high frequency reasons many folks respond to the TV Lawyers' commercials, since the inability to go to work will result in not getting a paycheck next payday, or for many paydays to come, depending upon how seriously injured you are. Not getting paid is another form of damages known variously by names such as *Lost Wages*, or *Lost Income*, or *Diminished Earning Capacity.*

No matter what you call it, it hurts. Few of us can go for long without money to live on. The tempting words of a *runner* promising money in advance for living expenses is hard for some to resist. What the runner doesn't tell you, is that what ever money you get from the lawyer, you will have to pay back. Most likely, if your lawyer collects any money for you, the money advanced or "loaned" to you will be deducted from the settlement funds. That's how you pay it back. The lawyer really should not be lending you money at all! When the lawyer advances money to a client it may be against the law. There is a thing called *champerty.* Seldom do some lawyers even give it a second thought. Why should they? How often do you hear about a lawyer getting punished for anything?

It was decided many years ago by men with wisdom and a sense of justice and fair play that to allow a lawyer to finance his client's lawsuit was inherently wrong. It puts the lawyer in the position of being an actual party to the lawsuit. The lawyer's interest should be clear and separate from the interests of his client. How can that be, if the lawyer has his own money invested in the lawsuit? There is a distinct conflict of interest established, and some would seriously question the lawyer's motives. Is the lawyer representing a client? Or, is he just operating a business in which he invests his money in the misery and misfortune of another for a profitable return? However it's done or whether you think it is okay or not, it is wrong.

So, if your motive for signing up with a lawyer is to get a loan from him, remember that banks are in the business of lending money. Lawyers should be practicing law and they should stay out of the banking business unless they want to buy stock in a bank. Many of them certainly have money enough to invest in bank stock since representing automobile accident victims is such a lucrative business. Hopefully, you will see this too, and not fall for the runner's misleading promises.

Brother, Can You Spare A Dime?

So, where do you get money to live on? Well, most folks will usually have some means of getting by. Your job may provide you with *workers' compensation* if you were injured on the job. Workers' Compensation insurance is a form of insurance developed as a form of *no fault* insurance. Coverage which pays accident victims' medical expenses, money to live on while they are disabled and in some cases *indemnity* or money for damages when the injury lasts for a very long time or is permanent. It is called no fault because an injured worker does not have to prove his employer was negligent and his employer cannot use the worker's own negligence as an excuse to get out of paying for his injuries. If you are injured on the job and you are not guilty of certain acts of *gross negligence*, you will be able to draw compensation, which is a portion of your regular weekly wage. Your medical expenses will be paid and if you have any residual permanent injury additional money will be paid to you for that.

The law which established workers' compensation has undergone many changes over the years and the rules under which a person can be said to have been injured "on the job" have been expanded considerably. For example, if you are assigned a company vehicle for regular use, that is, if you can even take it home with you at night, you may, if injured in an accident on your way home from work, be considered to have been injured *on the job*. If you are covered for workers' compensation, you need to try to find out if your injury could be considered as one eligible for this kind of protection. If it is, you can collect insurance money to keep things going while you heal.

Oh, and *gross negligence*? That is a different kind of negligence. Although in workers' comp it is not really gross negligence but certain specific violations, like being drunk on the job or intentionally injuring yourself, which may prevent you from collecting, gross negligence is something out of the ordinary. It may involve serious misconduct or even malicious intent. It is the judgement of society that your conduct is so bad that it requires special treatment as a deterrent for other folks, so they won't do the same thing. It is also the basis for paying *exemplary* or *punitive* damages - money given to an injured party for the stated purpose of punishing the wrong doer for his misconduct.

And then there is *disability* insurance. Insurance companies sell policies which provide coverage for a person whenever he is disabled from an accidental injury. It usually makes no difference if the accident or injury occurred on the job or not. Many people buy such coverage for themselves, especially if they know that there is no workers' compensation coverage available to them. Some, because of their position in a company, may have this kind of insurance provided for them by their businesses or employers. The policies usually pay a certain amount of money each day a person is disabled as a result of an injury sustained by accident.

One form of such insurance is found in the automobile policies which include *PIP*. You may recall this type of coverage from our discussion in Chapter Six. Personal Injury Protection pays for medical expenses and lost wages up to the limit of the policy, usually $2,500, but can be higher. The coverage applies to medicals and wages jointly not separately. By that I mean if your medical expenses are more than the limit, for example, more than $2,500, then you will have no money left available for lost wages. You will have this coverage available to you in one of two ways. If the vehicle which you were occupying at the time you were injured has this coverage on its policy, you will be eligible for those benefits. Or if you were in someone else's car at the time you were injured, and your car has PIP coverage, you will get help from PIP. In fact, if both cars have PIP, yours and the car in which you were injured, you can get payments from both cars if the total of your loss is greater than the coverage of one of them.

If your state is a so-called *No Fault* state, there should be insurance available to pay for your lost wages whether you were in your own car or some other person's car. It should pay regardless of which driver caused the accident. Of course, in those states there should be less incentive for a person to hire a lawyer in the first place, but people still do. I cannot help but wonder why. Why would anyone hire someone else to collect insurance money for them when the law of the state says they must be paid anyway? I don't get it!

When there is no insurance coverage of any kind available to you to pay your living expenses on a running basis while you are disabled, you must survive in some other fashion. Savings account, loans from friends and family and having other members of the family work while you are laid up are some of the things you must do to get by. And while we are talking about it, is there a question as to whether or how long you should take off work as a result of injuries sustained in an accident? Yes, there is.

Although some may think that the longer they take off from work, the bigger the claim settlement they will get, it may not be true. Consider this: your actual lost wages will, in most cases, be added to the evaluation of your claim on a dollar-for-dollar basis. You are entitled to recover only what you lost. If you don't get paid for a week's work, then payment in money equivalent to what you would have earned on the job will be paid to you by the insurance company in the settlement. Not three times your wages or anything else. Just the money you lost, nothing else. So staying off work does not increase the amount of money you are going to get and keep for yourself. It is what some call a zero sum game. It's six in and six out.

It is always in your best interest and in the best interest of your family for you to try to get back to work as soon as is reasonably possible considering the extent of your injury and how well you are healing. I know as well as you do that there are folks who think that being injured in an accident is their signal to go on permanent vacation. But it doesn't increase the value of their claim in any way, especially if it can be shown that the injury was not severe enough to warrant such an extended period of disability. There are still rules. Some of them benefit one side and some the other. If you try to mistreat the system, you are in for a rough time of it. You may find that the system will mistreat you.

Take advantage of sick leave time if you have it available. Even though you continue to get paid while out sick or injured, you will still be able to collect money from the insurance company to make up for the sick time you lose. If you have no sick time coming, or if your employer does not pay you for sick leave, take vacation days instead of losing a paycheck. Remember, as in the case of sick leave, you will still get paid for your vacation time if you had to take it because of injury sustained in an insurance protected accident.

I should mention that in extreme cases involving serious injury and/or permanent disability, seek help from some of the various government agencies which are in place to fill those special needs: The Veteran's Administration. Aid To Dependant Children. Or the Social Security Administration. Local charities, churches and relief organizations such as The Salvation Army often step in where there is no other help available. Don't make the mistake of letting your pride get in the way if you really need assistance. Just remember after it is all over to go back and contribute all you can to help others who may find themselves in similar circumstances.

A Day Late And A Dollar Short

The point I am trying to get to in this chapter is to describe how lost wages figure into your insurance claim. You should know that there are many ways for you to get the money you need to get by during any time you cannot work and cannot get paid. I hope these suggestions will help, but more importantly, how do lost wages count and how do you prove it?

All courts hold that if you are injured by someone and that injury causes you to lose income, you should be compensated by the person who caused your injury to the extent of your loss. That is to say, if you lose, as a result of your injury, $1,000 in wages, which you would have earned had you not been injured, you can collect a $1,000 from the person who hurt you. You must understand that credit for taxes will be considered. The $1,000 I was talking about is *take-home* pay. Your net income, after taxes.

Most adjusters will figure about 20 percent of gross income for taxes. Say your weekly salary is $500. Assume you are disabled and cannot work for one week. Your employer would have "paid" you a total of $500, but you would only have taken home about $400 of that because of taxes taken out of your paycheck. So, when your claim is calculated, $400 will be added to the settlement for lost wages, not $500. Since you are not required to pay taxes on insurance proceeds, collecting the full amount of your wages <u>before</u> taxes are taken out would actually allow you to make a profit on your loss. And, there is no reason to allow people to make a 20 percent profit on wages because of an accident. Insurance indemnity should not be a profit making venture. Compensation is all you should get, not enrichment.

Having said that, I encourage you to make the best deal you can. It is not your responsibility to deprive yourself of money in some noble effort to "right the system." There are different kinds of damages as was earlier pointed out and in those other kinds of damages you will find better ways of increasing the amount of insurance money you can collect than by trying to inflate your wage loss. You should inform yourself fully and do it correctly. And here's how. There are some simple rules to follow in gathering the information to prove lost wages. The easiest is when you work for an hourly wage and are paid on a regular basis such as every week or every other week.

Your adjuster will ask you for a wage loss verification authorization. He will ask you to sign a form. That form will be addressed to your employer. It will ask certain questions to establish if and when you were off work. It will ask the reason for your having missed working. How long you were off. Whether there is workers' compensation available to you. If you lost any wages and how much. The answers your boss gives back to the adjuster will determine how much money the adjuster will add to your settlement for lost wages. Give the adjuster the authorization. To do otherwise is to tell the adjuster you are not going to cooperate. Your only recourse then is to give some of your settlement money to a lawyer for giving the wage information to the adjuster for you. How dumb is that?

Salaries Count

Salaried people have a special problem. They will probably continue to get paid while off work due to an injury at least for a while. The typical situation is when a person is paid a regular salary on a monthly or yearly basis regardless of the number of hours they spend on the job. A person may earn $24,000 per year, or $2,000 per month, or even $500 per week. They get paid the same amount of money every pay day. It makes no difference if they work long hours or short. Whether they get sick or not. Whether they turn out as much work as their fellow workers or less. Of course, you realize that if they continue to underproduce for a long time, they will soon be on the unemployment rolls and get no salary at all, but for the sake of our discussion, assume that no matter what, they will get paid.

Okay, so you get a salary. You get hurt. You take off work a week or ten days. Next pay day, there is exactly the same amount of money in your paycheck as there was last payday! Wow, what a deal! Then you talk to the adjuster. The adjuster asks, "Did you lose any money as a result of your injury?" How do you answer? Do you say, "No, I got a bird's nest on the ground. My boss is so dumb he just keeps paying me whether I show up for work or not?" I hope you don't. So does your boss. Well, what <u>do</u> you say?

You tell him that you are salaried and that although you did not actually miss a paycheck, you were disabled to the extent that your *wage earning capacity* was diminished. Translation: "If you were not salaried, you would not have been able to earn any money at all during the period you were unable to work." That is worth, in insurance dollars, the same amount as though you had actually lost the wages. Don't let the adjuster screw you around. If he cannot agree to that without an argument, he is either a fool or a fraud - he is either stupid or dishonest. Either way, you need to hold his feet to the fire. You ARE entitled to collect a sum of money equal to the amount your injury caused you to lose, or would have caused you to lose, had some sort of guarantee of your wages not been available to you.

How do you prove this? Give the adjuster a wage verification authorization. Ask him to send it to your employer. Even though your employer may say you actually lost no wages at all, he will also tell the adjuster that you had to take off work for a period of time due to your injuries. Since this will also be backed up by your doctor in his report to the adjuster, the adjuster will have all the proof necessary to calculate your wage loss. It's really only arithmetic.

Pocket Calculator

Divide your salary for the period of time on which it is based. If you are paid an annual salary, divide it by 300. (That is the approximate number of actual working days in a year.) Don't let anyone divide it by 365 because you don't actually work that many days and that would reduce the daily wage rate unreasonably. Figure it out, you will see. If you are paid by the month, divide your monthly salary by 22 days. If you are paid by the week, divide your weekly salary by five working days. As an adjuster, I don't really care if a holiday falls in the week you were off work or not, unless you give me a hard time, and then I might even add up the actual **hours** you missed work.

You wanta see some numbers? Say you earn $500 per week. Your accident occurred Tuesday afternoon on your way home from work. The injury caused you to be off work the rest of that week and all of the following week. Divide your weekly salary of $500 by five. The result should be $100, if both our calculators are working properly. So, it can be said you earn $100 per day. You missed Wednesday, Thursday and Friday of the week your accident happened and five days the next week for a total of eight days. Multiply eight days by your daily wage rate of $100 and you get a total <u>gross</u> wage loss of $800. Don't forget the taxes.

Multiply your $800 wage loss by 20 percent and subtract that amount from the gross loss. $800 less $160 leaves $640. Since the injury made it impossible for you to work, the injury made it impossible for you to earn money during that period of time. Therefore, $640 is amount you are entitled to collect regardless of whether you actually got paid or not. The measure of how much, is the amount of the actual salary you would have earned, had you not been injured. Frankly, I would try to get the adjuster to pay the entire $800. Often they will, especially where the wage loss is not great.

You can supply the adjuster with copies of your paycheck stubs if they break down your wages showing all deductions. He can calculate the loss from that, but beware of any attempt to deduct things like insurance, payroll savings deductions or any non-tax item from the gross amount. Always figure it yourself first so you can check the adjuster's calculations to see if it is done right. Some adjusters are dummies, too. Even though you provide the adjuster with paycheck stubs, don't be surprised if you are also asked for a wage loss verification authorization form since the adjuster must still verify the loss with your employer.

It makes no difference whether you are paid a salary or by the hour or on commission as far as proving your loss goes. It gets a bit stickier for those who work for themselves. Your individual special situation will dictate how to prove your loss. The self-employed person who keeps good records should have no problem. Those who don't will have difficulty. But take heart, it can be done.

Good record keeping always serves the honest person well. Review your earnings over the past few weeks or months. Determine an average hourly, daily, weekly or monthly earnings rate.

Use that as the basis of figuring the wage loss. But, always include in your calculations all information about your expenses. After all, your actual income is what is left over after you subtract all of your expenses from the gross income. So, if you collected $800 for a job you did last week, don't divide that $800 by five. First subtract any and all expenses you incurred in earning the $800 before dividing by five. What might those expenses be? Cost of materials purchased to do the job. Cost of equipment rented. An amortized portion of the cost of equipment purchased to do the work. Gasoline to get to and from the job. Postage, paper, pencils, pots, pans and paraphanalia. In short, anything you had to spend in order to earn the $800 in the first place. Whatever is left over can be divided by five to arrive at your daily wage loss.

A simple report of these figures should do, but if the sum is substantial or if the adjuster insists on detailed verification, you may have to present actual receipts and other records to prove up the wage loss. You should know, there are other ways of proving lost wages or lost income opportunities. If you had a contract to do work during the period of disability which you were unable to fulfill because of your injury, provide proof by allowing the adjuster to interview the person you were to work for. Don't try to get written proof from the person yourself. Adjusters rarely believe such information is valid. They will almost always want to check it out for themselves.

It is always a good idea to inform your customer of your need to have him discuss the matter with your adjuster to avoid offending him and possibly cutting off a good source of supportive information and even future work. The same is true for people you have worked for in the past. When business is good and you are completing much work for a lot of people and an injury lays you low, use those past customers as references to prove to the adjuster how much you had regularly been earning prior to your injury. When you talk to such prior customers, make a quality control call out of it. Ask them about your work. Are they satisfied? Are there any problems? Can you do anything else for them? And, of course, will they talk to your adjuster for you?

Some self-employed tradesmen work through dispatchers of some kind. If any additional proof is needed by the adjuster, refer the adjuster to your dispatcher to show how much work you had been doing prior to your injury and how much you missed by not being able to work.

Lastly, if all else fails, you may have to provide the adjuster with copies of your last year's income tax reports. That method will give you an annual earnings report which you can divide by 300 days to get a daily wage loss rate. If you cannot prove your wage loss in any other way, please don't be offended by the adjuster's request. It is absolutely necessary to verify wage losses or the adjuster may not be able to get *settlement authority* from the insurance company with which to settle your claim. Fine, what the heck is *settlement authority*? The power or ability of every insurance adjuster to do anything is always limited to some degree by the insurance company for which he works. Whether a *staff* adjuster or *independent*, all work, whether investigation, analysis, evaluation or settlement, is controlled by the insurance company, the adjuster's *principal.* Oh boy, a bunch more terms to talk about! I love this stuff!

A staff adjuster is a person, male or female, who is employed as an insurance claim representative for a particular insurance company. Such adjuster does not work for any other company. Just one. All claims handled by a staff adjuster will be those filed against policies issued by his employer. An independent adjuster is an adjuster who works for himself or an independent adjusting firm who represents many different insurance companies. Staff adjusters tend to have *discretionary* settlement authority, meaning they always have some authority to settle claims on their own judgment without asking their supervisor for permission. Independent adjusters seldom have any authority whatsoever without getting special permission and/or instructions from the supervisor.

All adjusters are deemed to be *agents* of and act only on the authority of their principals, persons or entities who control the adjuster - tell the adjuster what to do and how far to go. The principal extends authority to settle a claim to an adjuster. It may be a discretionary amount of authority which the adjuster can use at will or it may be specific and limited authority granted for a specific purpose or single claim. But in either case, the adjuster cannot act on his own. He must have authority from the insurance company before he can act - to do anything. And in order to get settlement authority on your particular claim, the adjuster must have verification of all your damages. Otherwise, no deal.

And insofar as lost wages are concerned, you will be required to verify or provide proof of what you lost in order that it can be included in the evaluation of your claim. It's your money. Do whatever it takes to collect it.

10 One, Two, Three, Oh, How Elementary It's Gonna' Be

Figuring out how much your claim is worth is really just a matter of adding up your damages. Although it may not be as easy as you might like it to be, it is easier than you think it will be. It's a matter of basics and details. Do you know what a *Public Adjuster* is?

A Public Adjuster is a different kind of adjuster. He does not work for an insurance company. Neither does he work for an independent adjusting company which in turn works for insurance companies. The public adjuster offers his services to the general public. That's where the name comes from. Instead of representing an insurance company, the public adjuster represents an individual insured *against* the insurance company.

The public adjuster seeks out people who have sustained losses which are covered by insurance policies, usually *property* claims. Those are most often claims resulting from fires, floods and other catastrophic losses which have caused physical damage to homes and other buildings. A policyholder upon being contacted by a public adjuster may enter a contract with the public adjuster similar to the contract others sign with lawyers to represent them in their liability claims against others. Only in these cases, the claims are not liability claims. That is, they are not claims being made against other people, but claims which are being made against the insurance company which issued the policy covering the damaged property. This contract will give the public adjuster a portion of any money collected from the insurance company. The amounts vary from a low of 10 percent upwards to around 25 percent, according to the contract.

Unfortunately that is not all. In some cases the public adjuster may encourage the policyholder to participate in the inflation of the claim in such a way that the public adjuster gets an even larger share of the recovery. The trick is for him to get the policyholder as much as he would have collected from the insurance company any way, and get enough over that amount to satisfy his own desires. If the public adjuster does not substantially increase the amount of recovery to cover the cost of his service, he is cheating the insured in a way, since the insured could have gotten the same amount of money from the insurance company without using a public adjuster.

Now, how fair of a statement is that? Well, maybe not fair at all, if you are a public adjuster. But over all, public adjusters are even more unnecessary than lawyers! The number of claims where the services of a public adjuster are really needed is very small in relation to the number of cases in which they get involved. In many cases, the public adjuster serves no interest but his own. The same is true of many of the so-called plaintiff's lawyers. They insert themselves into the claim process for the sole purpose of raking off a portion of the insurance proceeds for themselves. They usually succeed in increasing the cost of insurance claims and they usually succeed in convincing their clients as to what a great job they did in making the insurance company pay.

The fact of the matter is, that most public adjusters, both the good ones and the lousy ones, always inflate the claim and cause the insurance company to pay out more money than they would have otherwise. Whether that is in the best interest of the people whom the public adjuster represents, I'm not so sure. I do know that in the vast majority of cases, a policyholder does not need a public adjuster to handle the claim. You can almost always get as much directly from the insurance company yourself as you will by hiring a public adjuster to collect it for you.

But it is important to understand why the public adjuster can drive the cost up so much. It is, in my opinion, a tribute to their skills to say that they can do it. The good public adjusters build their claim files from the ground up. They rely on the basics and they pay a great deal of attention to the smallest detail of the claim. The public adjuster overlooks NOTHING!

Repair estimates written on damaged houses by public adjusters are itemized to an extent most insurance adjusters regard as tedious. The repair operations are broken down into the smallest units possible. Even *unit costs* are reduced to their smaller components whenever possible. *Unit cost* is the term applied to a figure used in preparing estimates which includes materials, labor, hardware and incidental items instead of listing each of those separately. An estimate will show, for example, that painting a wall will cost $.30 per square foot. That is the unit cost - $.30/SF. Actually that figure represents the cost of the paint, cleaners, thinners, brushes, drop cloths, masking materials and labor for the painter and his helper.

The public adjuster will use unit costs in writing the estimate, but he will apply the unit cost to more than just the wall itself. The estimate will show the cost of painting the wall, painting the base trim around the bottom of the wall, painting the trim around the door in the wall and any windows in the wall. It will include such items as removing the covers from the electrical switches and plug-in outlets. It will show masking of the ceiling, if the ceiling's color is different from the wall. It will often include preparing the wall for the painting process, which normally is included within the unit cost of painting itself.

The public adjuster includes every single itemizeable thing he can think of when writing the repair estimate. The result is almost always a total estimated cost of repairs much higher than would have been reached following the standard methods used by insurance adjusters and building contractors. Well, I don't want to go on, but I do want you to understand that the public adjuster does his homework and does it well. YOU should do the same.

The elementary basics of calculating the value of anything, including insurance claims, begin with 1, 2, 3. COUNT EVERYTHING! Start with one and add another. Then add another, and another until you get to the end of what you're counting. It works exactly the same way in placing a value on your bodily injury claim.

Hooray, For The Public Adjuster!

No matter what you call the damages, they all add up to insurance money you can collect without a lawyer (or a public adjuster, for that matter). But before we get too far away from public adjusters, let me say this about them, there IS a need. Although P.A.'s don't really need justification any place except in the insurance industry's world, it is only fair to point out the reasons for their existence. Perhaps in the beginning, public adjusters served a very real need in helping policyholders prepare their claims in commercial losses. Very large losses are difficult, if not impossible, for an individual policyholder to present. Commercial losses can sometimes, and often do, involve extensive inventories of goods. Some large and commercial buildings can require the services of not only a building contractor but an engineer or even an architect to figure out how to repair the damage. There are also cases where the individual policyholder needs assistance, although these are much rarer.

If everything is done properly and on time, the insurance adjuster's duties include all of these things and the cost should be paid by the insurance company. But unluckily, adjusters also come in many different flavors. There are insurance adjusters who are lazy. Some are not well-trained. Some are incompetent, some are dishonest and some are downright stupid! It is because of just such adjusters that public adjusters do well. If the adjuster can't or won't do his job right, then I think the policyholder needs help. If the choice of help is a public adjuster, that is the insurance company's tough luck! They should do a better job, a more prompt job, a more thorough job. They should send people out to see their policyholders instead of having someone call the insured on the telephone and try to "guess" at what the customer's problems and needs are.

In far too many cases, the insurance companies and their adjusters don't and that is why we have so many active public adjusters. Sorry, Mr. Insurance Executive, but you and your actuaries have brought it on yourselves! Maybe the greatest contribution of the public adjuster is in keeping the insurance companies on their toes. It is important for there to be some balance in the market place to offset the arrogance of some insurance companies and some insurance people. If the public adjuster does no more than that, he is a welcome addition to our community.

Know Your Job -

But, back to damages. We have already discussed damages in Chapter Six, you know, Special damages, General Damages, Exemplary or punitive damages. Since you will not be required to pass the bar exam, don't dwell on this too much, but special damages can be considered as those easily proven in specific dollar amounts. Things you will have bills and receipts for. Those that you will be able to prove with written documents of some kind, such as letters, forms and pay stubs. Special damages include your doctor bills, hospital bills, drug store receipts for prescription medicines, ambulance bills, therapy bills. They include receipts for crutches, walkers, traction devices. Gasoline for driving to and from the doctor's office or to the therapist's. The cost of broken eyeglasses is another item, easily itemized and proven with hard copies of paper. That cost, too, is among the things you may include in your special damages. OVERLOOK NOTHING!

So, how about General Damages? General damages are not so easily proven. They include things which are difficult to measure in money terms. The pain you feel as a result of being injured - how much is it worth? Who knows? When you are feeling it, there may be no price you would accept to continue to suffer that pain. To the injured person, his pain is worth millions. To the insurance company which is being asked to pay the claim, that same pain may be worth very little. This is the stuff that makes horse races. They are arguable but, better yet, negotiable.

General damages may include pain. They may include suffering. They may include anxiety. They may include *loss of consortium*, which usually means not being able to have sex with your partner because of an injury sustained in an accident. That is, of course, not all loss of consortium is. It is really the loss of the comfort and benefit of having a close and dear partner to give you warmth, happiness, advice and many other things. General damage might include your not being able to attend your grandfather's funeral or your daughter's graduation because of an injury sustained in an accident. Anything, in short, which cannot easily be measured in dollars and cents can be regarded as general damages. It is ironic that the task of an insurance claim settlement is to do just that, measure the damages in terms of dollars and cents.

The most dollars and cents in claim payments result from punitive damages. These are the payments taken from a wrong doer as punishment. You will probably not be able to do much with this one. It requires showing that the bad guy was *really* bad! The negligence involved must show a degree of malice or gross failure to perform reasonably in order to collect punitive damages. You probably need a lawyer for that. But if you are interested in collecting as much insurance money as you can, you're better off sticking with special and general damages which you can collect on your own. Punishment is not very satisfying anyway. Unless you are talking in hundreds of thousands of dollars or millions, how good can it feel? Stick to what you can do.

Keeping Track Of Things -

What you can do is keep track of every single item of expense whether the money is spent or not. I mean, if you get estimates of future medical treatments which will or may become necessary, get written evidence of those items and save them as well. Your first expense might be a bill from an ambulance service. Some volunteer medical service organizations will not bill you unless they know insurance is involved. Let them know and ask them for a bill. That serves a dual purpose of helping to increase the amount you can collect from the insurance company and it helps the volunteer medical service unit with their budgets.

The next item may be a statement from a hospital or other emergency medical service provider for attending to your injuries before a regular treating doctor can get to you. These may be followed up by hospital bills, prescription medicines, collars and any of hundreds of other devices used by doctors and hospitals to treat accident victims. Believe me, the hospital will "stick" it to you in more ways than one. So, be careful. Their bills can be questioned by the adjuster. Excess charges, duplicate charges, erroneous charges often show up on hospital bills. A sharp adjuster will catch these items and ask that they be eliminated from consideration as part of your claim.

How do you get home from the hospital? Another ambulance? Another bill! Will you require nursing care after you return home? If so, all such expenses become a part of your special damages. More importantly, they become a part of that magical arithmetical figure that you get to multiply by three to get where you're going! Isn't that great? Well, it is, you'll see.

The doctor will want you to come to the office for follow-up examinations. You will have to get there some way. No matter whose car you use to get to the doctor's office, it will burn gasoline or some other type of fuel. That fuel costs you money, so get a receipt and keep track of the mileage. That is also a part of your special damages along with Band-Aids, aspirin, "Que sticks," lotions, antiseptics, dressings and beer. No, not beer. I just wanted to see if you were paying attention.

Overlook nothing! The more detail you include in your presentation to the adjuster the more likely it is that you will recover the amount of money you desire. The basic elements, counted one by one, will grow into provable special damages which will become intimidating during settlement negotiations. There is a book written by Robert Ringer called, "Winning Through Intimidation." The name of the book is sort of intimidating itself. Mr. Ringer's point is that you make yourself strong by doing careful and thorough homework, that when you have sufficient information, carefully organized and that when you are totally prepared before beginning any negotiation, you will seem to overpower your opposition. That is exactly what you should do when getting ready to deal with the insurance adjuster about your claim. And the time to begin is immediately.

So, save everything. Every bill, every statement, every letter, every receipt. Every report. Every estimate. Every prediction by your doctor. Save it all, and keep it in good order. As a minimum requirement, at least place them all in a folder, or a box or even a paper bag properly marked. But you should keep a running record for yourself. An inventory of all of your expenses in the order in which you got them. Later, when you begin to add up everything and try to place a value on your claim, you will have saved yourself much time and trouble.

Don't overlook your property damage claim either. Keep track of wrecker bills, towing and storage charges, repair estimates, repair work orders and bills. Carefully save all information about any rent car you used or other substitute transportation. If the car was a total loss, of course, keep all the information you gathered about the value of the car and the actual cost of replacing it. Keep the property damage receipts separate from your bodily injury receipts. The adjuster will not let you lump everything together. He must keep those two major categories separate.

If you've done all that, you can start to put together a picture of your general damages. Your inability to earn wages. Your inability to perform routine daily tasks or to carry on with a hobby (or with your hubby) all count as a part of your general damages. Many elements make up the profile of your general damages. Who you are, makes a difference. The lifestyle you followed prior to your injury makes a difference. The neighborhood in which you live can influence the outcome of your claim - both up and down. Living in a poor neighborhood does not necessarily mean you will get less money, it may mean you will get more. Living in a high dollar, ritzy neighborhood could decrease the money you collect as well as increase it.

You need to put together a story about yourself which will tell the adjuster that because of your special circumstances, whatever they happen to be, you are entitled to more money than the last claimant or the next. Are you a single mother? Did you not only have working problems, but baby sitting problems as well? That is worth money. Are you disabled? Confined to a wheel chair? That may change your story sufficiently to cause an adjuster to pay you a little more. And, PLEASE, don't look at that as using a disadvantage as an unfair advantage. It's all a part of the money game. And the money game is what you're playing when you try to collect insurance money whether you use a lawyer, a public adjuster or just do it yourself.

Painting A Picture -

There was an old television commercial - I don't even remember the product being advertised - I do remember there being some dirty jokes made out of it - which closed with the line, "Mother - please, I'd rather do it myself!" Said with feeling, of course. Well, that is what you should still be saying to yourself now, "I would rather do it myself, than give a third to a half of my money away." The way to do that is to make yourself powerful and intimidating by gathering up as much information as you can. Organize it into chronological as well as logical order. Keep a log of your expenses and experiences. Paint an insurance claim portrait of yourself, using every advantage you can to make your claim look as valuable as possible. I promise, the adjuster will be doing everything possible to make your claim look as though it's worth much less.

Don't believe me, huh? Remember that wheelchair we talked about above? I recall a claim made by a young lady who had been confined to a wheel chair for many years. This was before the days when society encouraged especially challenged people to get out and get active. Those were the days when folks just believed that if you were unlucky enough to find yourself in a wheel chair, you should resign yourself to it and stay home. This girl was not employed. But she had a hobby making little creatures out of paper clips, hairpins, string and paper. She made them first for her own pleasure, but soon began making them for relatives and friends. Because she was injured while a passenger in the back seat of a car when it was struck by a pickup truck which ran a red light, she could not continue her hobby. She recovered and was able to return to the hobby later, but during that period of time which she could not, she was entitled to some consideration for her loss of the ability to do it.

The adjuster denied all but her actual provable special damages because she was a wheel chair victim! He reasoned that since she had been unable to get out of the house and hold down a job before the accident, she was not entitled to collect any damages for the temporary disability imposed on her by the injury. (This young lady <u>should</u> have hired an attorney, but she didn't). Fortunately, she had the good sense to pick up the telephone and ask to speak to the adjuster's supervisor. And although she still did not get the consideration she really deserved, at least some payment was made for the disability which caused the temporary loss of her hobby.

Know Thine Enemies -

What's my point? My point is that the insurance companies will use whatever they can against you. So, when trying to collect insurance money, you should wise up and use everything you can against the insurance companies. Think about who you are. Paint a portrait of yourself as an insurance claimant. Answer these questions. Where do you live? What kind of education do you have? What kind of work do you do? Where do you work? What kind of car do you drive? How do you dress?

It all matters. Even your physical condition, whatever it is. What language you speak. What dialect you speak. (Dialect shows up in your voice based on what part of the country you grew up in) Do you speak the slow, flattened vowel sound of a southerner? Do you speak the rapid sharp talk of a northeasterner? It all matters.

Do you drink alcohol? Do you smoke cigarettes? Are you single, married, divorced, abandoned, hated, popular, unpopular? Paint this insurance portrait of yourself and then take stock of that portrait. HOW WAS IT CHANGED BY THE INJURY YOU SUSTAINED IN YOUR ACCIDENT? The way and extent of change is the yardstick by which you measure general damages. And anybody's guess as to how much general damages are worth is as good as anyone else's. Remember, your estimate of the value of that part of your claim is probably just as good as the adjuster's, although you may not agree with one another.

In placing a value on your claim, be realistic as well as practical. Don't decide your claim is worth a million dollars, because it probably is not. If it were, no doubt you would need a lawyer to prove it. Think about how much money you had before the accident. Consider how much you were earning before the accident. Remind yourself of how sensitive <u>you</u> are to pain. But be honest. And probably the most important of all, ask yourself how much would it take to satisfy you. To what would you say yes, if the adjuster made you an offer of settlement? That is the approximate value of your claim. But we're getting ahead of ourselves, here. You will also need reports.

11 Happy (Paper) Trails To You

You need to complete building your paper trail with *Official Reports*. These are the reports filed, in connection with your accident, by governmental agencies. Police accident reports, medical reports, fire marshall's reports and ambulance reports are among the types of written documents you may need to prove your claim. Many of these will be completed and filed by a person working for a government unit of some kind. It may be a police officer, a fire marshall, or an emergency medical attendant employed by the city or county where you live. You need to know where to get those reports and why. You need to know what impact the reports may have on your claim. This is all a part of your record keeping process which builds toward the proof and evaluation of your claim.

Let's start with police accident reports. If a peace officer such as city policeman, sheriff's deputy, constable, highway patrolman or state police officer investigates the accident, a report will be filed. The report will include much of the information we have already covered. But the information is recorded from the investigating officer's point of view. That view should be a neutral one. In other words, the officer should neither be biased for nor prejudiced against either side. If the officer is truly neutral, the report of the investigation will be very valuable and may make the difference to an adjuster whether the claim should be paid or not.

Bias And Prejudice -

Well, welcome to the real world. Police officers are not saints. You probably knew that already. There are white officers and black officers. There are Hispanic officers and Anglo officers. There are female officers and male officers - and some in between. Police officers come from varied backgrounds. Some come from poor families, some from wealthy families. Some have good educations obtained in high-quality schools and school districts, while some just barely got through a public school in a poor district with too few teachers, little discipline and lousy attitudes all around.

Accidents involve the same kind of people, as drivers, passengers, pedestrians and witnesses. White, black, Hispanic, Anglo, male, female, rich, poor, smart, not-so-smart, smart-aleck and lousy attitudes all around. You can well imagine the possible consequences of a white officer investigating an automobile collision between a black male driver and a pretty, young ,white female driver! Let's give the black guy a bad attitude to boot. How do you think that accident report is going to look? Do you think the black guy stands the chance of a snow ball in hell of getting a fair report? Well, it can happen, but I wouldn't count on it.

The point is, that people, all people, have built-in prejudices, biases and other mental baggage which they bring to every event of their lives. They interpret the world within their heads in strange and private ways. Sometimes they let these background feelings cloud their judgment. It can severely affect the outcome of an investigation and the completion of any report covering that investigation. Since you are reading this book, you have probably already been in an accident and it may be too late to suggest how to act at the accident scene. But if you are ever in an accident in the future and there are police officers on the scene, use your head. Be courteous. Be patient. Follow the officer's instructions. Answer the questions. Don't shoot your mouth off. Don't argue with the officers. And if you naturally have a bad attitude, try to hide it for the time being. The impression you make on the police officers at the scene of the accident may have more to do with the successful collection of insurance money than you think.

Travelogue -

If the accident is investigated by a city police department, you will need to go to the records or accident division of your local police to obtain a copy of the report. The reports are always available to you as a driver involved in the accident. There will be a fee from $1.00 to $10.00 for the report depending on the size of your city and the number of pages in the report. In large metropolitan areas, there may be more than one location where the reports are turned in or kept on file. Call your city police department. They will tell you where and how to get the report.

If the accident occurs outside the city limits in a county or parish area, it will probably have been investigated by the sheriff, one of the deputies or constables. The accident report will, in most areas, be available at the sheriff's office, the court house or the county records building. Again in large metropolitan areas, a county or parish report may be available at substations scattered about the county. You may have to call to find out which office has the report. When you call, ask how much it will cost and exactly what you must do to get a copy of the report. Some locations accept checks, some only cash. Some accept only the exact change. If the report costs $4.00, you may not be able to get it with a five-dollar bill expecting to get a one dollar bill in change. In such case, you must bring 4 one-dollar bills with you to get the report.

Accidents investigated by highway patrol, state trooper or state police present special problems. It is sometimes difficult to find out exactly when and where the accident report will be turned in. If there is a state police or highway patrol office in your area, call them for assistance. They will tell you where to go, how much it will cost and exactly what you must do to get a copy of the accident report.

It may seem like a lot of trouble to go to. But if you are going to succeed in this effort, having a copy of the accident report will be extremely helpful to you. The adjuster is supposed to get the report, and if your car is insured, the adjuster assigned to investigate the accident for your company should get a copy of the report. Ask. If one is available, the adjuster will probably make you a copy for free.

Some states keep all the automobile accident reports on file at the state capital. If that is the case in your state, you will be able to get a copy of the report by writing to the appropriate state office to request a copy. There may still be a charge, but you can probably pay it by check. Some states require that you submit an accident report to a state agency such as the Department of Public Safety on any accident in which someone is injured or there is property damage in excess of $100. It may be referred to by a nickname such as "Blue Form" or other short slang way of describing it. The proper police agency will tell you if such a report is necessary. But even if it is, that will not do you much good with the adjuster, even though it may be informative. After all, it is your report and may be self-serving.

Fires sometimes result from automobile accidents. In fact, the claim you are making might even be the result of injuries you sustained in a fire of some kind or other. Fire victims suffer extremely painful, debilitating and disabling injuries from fires whether it occurs as a result of an automobile collision or a house fire. Anytime the fire is the result of someone's negligence, the person injured has a valid claim against the person who caused the fire. And, if their negligence is covered by an insurance policy, the person injured will have a good opportunity to collect insurance money in connection with those injuries.

All fire departments file reports. The report may be by the unit or units which were dispatched to extinguish the fire. If the fire has a suspicious origin, a fire investigator might be assigned to determine the cause and origin of the fire. The Fire Marshall's office might look into the matter to find out if there is any possibility of arson. In any case, reports will be filed as a result of those inquiries. You may find a need to obtain copies of any such reports.

Top Secret!

You should know that some of those investigative reports will not be made available to you. Some of them are kept in strict confidence, especially if there is any chance of filing charges against a suspected arsonist. Sometimes they will allow you to have the front of a report but not the back or second pages. Short of a *court order* or *subpoena,* you will not get copies of any such protected reports. No doubt you understand what a court order is. It is simply a set of instructions issued by a judge telling someone that they must do something or face prosecution. A subpoena is much the same thing, but it is usually used to force someone to release evidence or to attend a trial or other judicial proceeding.

In spite of Freedom of Information laws, many bureaucrats will obstinately refuse to provide you with copies of documents clearly covered by the law. They do so because they are bureaucrats. They do so because they can, and that's the way they "get off." You see, if there is no proceeding filed in court, you cannot get a subpoena. So, without a lawyer AND a lawsuit, no subpoena, no records. What are you gonna' do? Nothing, go on to something else, something more productive.

Fire departments frequently, especially in large cities, provide ambulance service and emergency medical technicians to the community. When those folks come out to an accident scene, they are required to file reports of their activities. The technicians are usually well trained and are knowledgeable. They are especially observant and often make very good witnesses to the events which follow accidents. They often overhear conversations which include remarks and comments which point to the guilt or innocence of parties involved.

And, they can report on the condition of accident victims. Sometimes what an ambulance attendant says can rule out the existence of an injury which might later be claimed. And it is just as likely that the attendant might help you prove the existence and severity of your injury. Such reports are available from the fire department office out of which the ambulance or emergency medical personnel are supervised.

City or county engineering departments have a wealth of information at their disposal in regard to accident scenes and the condition of streets and roads. They may help you reconstruct the scene as it appeared at the time of your accident, even though it has since been changed by widening or other construction changes. Reports available from these departments can sometimes help you resolve disputes about the exact conditions which existed at the time of your accident. Or the exact time sequence of a traffic signal light as it changes from red to green to amber to red and so forth. There are times which information about the sequence of traffic light changes can make dramatic differences in the outcome of an investigation into accidents. It could make the difference between when you can collect insurance money and when you cannot.

Competition Is Good For - What?

In addition to official reports, you will need copies of damage repair estimates, medical reports and wage loss verification. You may get a repair estimate for the damage to your car from your adjuster, from the adjuster for the other driver, from a body shop which you have selected to repair your vehicle or a number of body shops if you or the insurance company want *competitive bids*. For bids to be competitive, they must be obtained honestly and they usually are not obtained that way. More often than not, the owner of a car will ask his body shop operator to get the so-called competitive bids for him. Many body shops keep pads of estimates printed for their competitors for just such occasions. Typically, after the shop writes his own estimate, he then makes two or three or more estimates on his competitors' estimate blanks, folds them differently and gets them a little dirty for "authenticity" and gives them to you as "competitive bids."

Whether you do it this way or not is up to you, but I still urge you to be honest and straightforward about these things. There is enough money to be made with a clear conscience. You don't have to cheat. In fact, if you ever find yourself in a situation where the body shop is getting extra estimates for you, put your hand on your wallet, because the body shop is about to get their hands into it. If you are asked to get two or three repair estimates, take advantage of the opportunity to shop around. Get the best price available and check the quality of the shops while you're at it.

If your claim arises out of damage to property other than an automobile such as a house, follow the same procedures but with building contractors instead of body shops. One comment is in order here. If you are making a claim for damage to your house, it will most likely be under your own policy, unless someone else damaged the house and there is insurance to cover it. When making claims against your own insurance company, keep in mind that your insurance company owes you duties some other insurance company doesn't. Your adjuster should be working for you. You have a right to expect more from your own company's adjuster including a prompt inspection of the damage and early completion of a repair estimate.

If your adjuster shows up with a contractor, ask why. The adjuster should be able to write his own estimate. If he can't, why not? Is he stupid or just lazy? Or worse, is he dishonest? You may want to check to see if he and his contractor friend spend weekends on the lake together. I want you to know these things in order that you may be able to protect yourself from the stupidity, greed and carelessness which characterize the handling of so many insurance claim matters today. If you are blessed with a competent, conscientious, honest adjuster, hallelujah! There are many of them out there. In fact, I must add that I believe most adjusters are well-trained and sincere in the desire to do the best job for you they can. But there are many of the other kinds out there too, so watch out!

Herbie's Doctor School -

Finally, medical reports, the reports made by your doctor or doctors, which describe your injury. The *diagnosis, treatment* and *prognosis* in connection with the injury. Here is a bunch of new words again. Ain't this fun? (I know some reader is now thinking, "Does this guy think <u>I'm</u> stupid?" No, I don't, but what am I going to write if I don't write this stuff?) The doctor's diagnosis of a condition, whether it be an injury, sickness or disease, is his evaluation and description of the condition. It is in short, the doctor's way of naming what is wrong with you. You have a cold. Or you have an upper respiratory infection, which is also a cold. You have a broken leg. Well, I think you get the point. The diagnosis is the result of finding out what ails you. Treatment is the procedures you and your doctor will follow together to correct the condition in order to get you back to good health or to "get well" again.

The doctor's prognosis is his prediction of what will happen to you in the future in so far as your injuries are concerned. The reports, when written in "doctorese" or "medicalese," will say things like, "The prognosis is guarded." That is probably the favorite of all time. What the doctor is saying is that he or she is unwilling to say anything definitive about the patient's condition. That way the lawyer can make the severity of the claim look like anything he wants. "Guarded" means that the patient could be well and healthy or it could mean that death is imminent! The doctor should tell us what the patient can expect in the future. Is the patient looking forward to extensive additional treatment? Will the patient recover completely? Will the patient need to continue treatment on an outpatient basis? How long will the patient need to receive treatment? How many additional treatments are expected? Will the patient have some remaining disability at the end of treatment? Will the patient be totally disabled? Will the patient LIVE?

Trouble For The Doc -

The prognosis should include the anticipated length and type of treatment, an estimate of the additional cost and what the patient's condition will be at the end of treatment. That doesn't sound too difficult, does it? Well, it can be. The doctors face a problem of their own in regard to insurance claims. It is called *malpractice*. Mal, meaning bad. The lawyers like to call it "mal feasance." That's very "lawyerish." It means, in short, that the doctor is being accused of doing a bad job in treating his patient. If a person can accuse his doctor of doing a lousy job in treating him, he can bring a claim against the doctor and, of course, his insurance company.

Such claims are often made for huge sums of money. You see, if you are not wealthy and have no insurance, you can probably run over someone in the street and never be required to pay them anything. But if that injured person should go to a doctor for treatment and later make a malpractice claim against the doctor, his otherwise worthless claim can suddenly turn into a claim worth hundreds of thousands of dollars! It has nothing to do with how the person got hurt and who is really liable to him for his injuries. It has only to do with money. It depends on who has the money and how much is available. The uninsured driver probably has no money or other assets. The doctor may be well off and, in addition, probably has malpractice insurance to cover his boo-boos.

What would you say in a report if every word you write opens you up to a law suit by someone for saying the wrong thing. Wrong does not necessarily mean that what the doctor says is wrong, just that some lawyer can make it look as though the doctor should not have said it. If the doctor says the patient will recover with no residual disability and the lawyer sends the patient to another doctor who finds that the patient needs extensive additional treatment and will be severely handicapped for the rest of his natural life, what do you think will happen next? A claim will be brought against the first doctor for what he said in the medical report. Unfortunately it makes little difference which doctor is fibbing and which is telling the truth. If the patient's lawyer can show that the patient was damaged in some way by what the first doctor said, Whammo!

So don't expect candor in a report from a doctor. Don't expect simple everyday language. You may feel that you need to buy a medical dictionary to interpret the report. You should ask the doctor to explain to you in laymen's language exactly what his report says and means. Make notes for yourself if you must, but make sure you understand what the doctor is saying about your injuries, the treatment you obtained and what the future has in store for you in connection with those injuries. The impact of the report on the adjuster can be great, indeed.

The adjuster will base his evaluation of your claim, in part, on what the doctor says about you in his report. The doctor should also tell if you are, have been or will be disabled for any period of time due to your injuries. This is a very important point if you have a claim for lost wages or lost income. Eyebrows will be sharply raised when you tell the adjuster your claim includes a month's lost wages, and the doctor's report says that you were off work for about three days! Make the doctor get it right. If a suggestion is made that you rest at home or in bed for any period of time, ask your doctor to do what AT&T asks MCI to do: Put it in writing. The note from the doctor will serve as an explanation of absence to your boss and proof of your lost income claim to the adjuster.

Daddy's Home To Stay -

Future disability is an important aspect of any personal injury claim. Disabilities can be partial or total. They can be temporary or permanent. They can be described in percentages, such as a temporary disability of 30 percent. Of course, the worst and the most expensive from a claim payment point of view is the 100 percent total and permanent disability. You'd think that a guy would almost have to be dead to get that prognosis, wouldn't you? It ain't necessarily so. Imagine a male worker, age 42, not so bright, but big and strong, who works in a steel mill. It is the only job the man has ever had. He knows nothing else. Remember. He's not so smart. Retraining would be difficult. Now, put him in an accident. His back is injured. Create a condition in his spinal column that will prevent him from bending easily, stooping over, lifting, twisting, turning or any other heavy or extreme physical exertion.

This man will lose his ability to earn a living. He will not be able to perform his old job and it is unlikely that he will be able to get another. He will get well. He will be able to play with his grandchildren. He can probably look forward to mowing the grass in his yard with a power mower. He will most likely be able to continue having sex with his wife. BUT! HE WILL BE TOTALLY AND PERMANENTLY DISABLED as far as the law is concerned. Okay, okay, I know, I've drawn an extreme example here, but such things happen.

A typist who blisters his finger cannot type. If he gets paid for typing, he will be unable to work and unable to earn money until the blister heals completely. A telephone equipment installer who has a muscle strain in the neck will be unable to lift, move about, adjust or install anything bigger than a paper clip. She will be unable to work and unable to earn a living until the muscles heal completely. Both of these people will have temporary periods of total disability. They may have a period of partial disability as the injuries heal during the recovery process. Both have valid and substantial claims for damages IF the injuries they sustained were caused by accident and another person's negligence caused the accident.

The results of injuries may be obvious to all, but you need a physician's report to back you up with the adjuster. When reviewing the adjuster's file, no one will be able to see you at home watching television during working hours. But if there is a medical report in the file which describes your injuries, explains what treatment is necessary and what treatment you are getting AND points out that you cannot work because of the injuries, most of the battle is over.

Go To The Doctor, Go To The Doctor Not. Go To The . . . -

What if you don't go to a doctor? If you are hurt, go see a doctor! Aside from the fact that it may be extremely dangerous for you to ignore any injury, why should anyone believe that you are injured if you don't get medical attention? Why should anyone believe that you were forced to take off work due to accidental injuries if you are not concerned about it enough to get down to Doc Whatizname's office for an examination and treatment? There must be a Doc Whatzername somewhere as well. The rule is always, if you think you have been injured, see a doctor. Countless times during my career folks have asked me, "Should I see a doctor?" My reply has always been, "Were you injured?" I always add, "If you are hurt, you need to see a doctor."

And, of course, after you see a doctor, always get a report from the doctor in writing. It makes little difference as to what form the medical report takes. The information it contains is the only thing of importance. It can be a fill-in-the-blank *Physicians and Surgeons Report* or it can be a multi-page typewritten or computer produced book-of-the-month type of report. The doctor can write it Lincoln style on the back of an envelope if he likes, as long as human beings can read it! It's what the report says that matters, not the form or beauty of the report. But the importance of the report cannot be overstated. Without it, you will encounter great difficulty in collecting insurance money. You can collect without a lawyer, but it is unlikely that you would have much of a chance at collecting without a medical report.

You should not overlook any official report available to you. Get them all. Make yourself intimidating by the power of the evidence you have to show to the insurance adjuster. In the somewhat modified words of one of our great men, "Walk softly, but carry a big pile of paper with you," when you go to see the money man. Do your homework. Be as detailed as possible. Gather the same information a lawyer would and based on the injuries and damages you sustained, collect as much insurance money as you can. And keep it all for yourself!

12 Peek-a-boo, I See You!

At the beginning of my career, while I was in claim school, an instructor told us of a claim which the company had investigated in California some years earlier. It involved an accident in which a man was injured while occupying an automobile at the time it was struck from the rear by another car. The man did not appear to be hurt at all as a result of the accident. However, he reported, to the insurance adjuster handling the file, that he had, in fact, been injured in the accident. This nameless claimant said that he had sustained a *whiplash!* That dreaded word! Do you know what whiplash is? It is a crick in the neck. Well, maybe a little more than that, but in essence it is a strain of some or one of the muscles in the neck. When you have one, it feels much like a crick in the neck. The treatment for it is the same. Mostly, you need rest, heat, relaxation and some aspirin. Now don't go telling me I'm practicing medicine, I've already told you, I'm not a doctor. But in my opinion, aspirin or some other household pain reliever is called for in these cases.

If you avoid any further strain for a while, the muscle will repair itself and you can go about your life again. But in the insurance world that crick in the neck becomes a medical disaster and a legal windfall. I believe that more money has been paid needlessly on claims for so-called whiplash injury in this country than on any other single type of injury. **Lawyers love it!** And I don't blame them. If I could ever find anything which would rake in that much loot for me, I would be thrilled too! To be fair, it should be noted that the range of *soft tissue injuries* is great. One person can sustain an injury to their neck or back which will give them only slight discomfort for a few days. Another can sustain what appears to be a similar injury and experience a lengthy hospital stay and a long recovery period. And yet another might have to undergo serious, dramatic and disabling surgery to correct the problem. The doctors know better than I.

The Plot Thickens -

Anyway, when a claimant says he has whiplash, the adjuster had better pay attention and investigate the matter thoroughly and properly. Our man in California said he had sustained whiplash. I forget now exactly what the man did for a living, but he was prevented, he said, from doing it, whatever it was. He did miss a lot of time from work. He stayed home every day. Or so it seemed. Whenever the adjuster would visit, and in those days adjusters actually did go out and see people, the claimant would be at home. Always, he would be wearing his neck brace. His traction device was always obviously in attendance. Prescription bottles adorned the table next to his lounge chair and his family doted on him. Everyone was concerned for his well being.

Although I do not recall his regular job, I do know what his avocation was. His hobby. He was an amateur wrestler. Whether he has strictly amateur or semi-professional, I don't know. But he did earn money wrestling. That is the important point. Because of his injury, he could no longer wrestle. Since he could no longer wrestle, he was losing substantial sums of money as a result of his neck injury. Proving the loss of income was difficult. He had no records to speak of. He could not or would not give any information to identify his boss, although he did refer the adjuster to a person reported to be an official of the wrestling federation. This person, not surprisingly, turned out to be a friend of his, whose only contact with the wrestling federation was when he watched the claimant wrestle.

Things just didn't add up right. The adjuster was curious, as he should have been. After consulting with his supervisor, the adjuster obtained permission to hire a professional undercover investigator. This investigator was equipped with *surveillance* cameras and other related tools. His assignment was to covertly watch the claimant for a period of time and to photograph his activities. The assignment included the taking of motion pictures, as well. I do mean motion pictures. There were no video cameras or tape in those days.

Weekdays were uneventful. The only times the claimant came out of the house, he wore his cervical collar (that means 'neck' collar). He was, more often than not, assisted by his wife. He never drove the car, but always sat in the right front passenger's seat. And at times, it could be seen that he appeared to be in some degree of discomfort.

A Breakthrough!

But on the weekends! Early one Saturday morning the investigator was pouring coffee from his thermos jug trying to wake himself up, when he noticed activity at the claimant's house. Not too concerned at first, he had to scramble a bit to get his movie camera going when he realized that the claimant was leaving the house. The investigator followed in his disguised panel truck as the claimant and his wife headed south on the highway. After a drive of about two hours, they arrived in the southern California town where the claimant's fortunes were about to take a turn for the worse.

Climax!

The claimant, not having been satisfied with the settlement offers made to him by the adjuster, had hired a lawyer. The lawyer, having feigned being insulted by the adjuster's offers, had filed a lawsuit. The trial date was at hand and the lawyer's most recent settlement demand was enormous. The facts were clear. The insurance company's policyholder had rear-ended the claimant at a red light. No hope there. The medical reports were very damaging. The claimant's doctor predicted that the man might never be able to wrestle again. His future earnings loss would be substantial. The company would be lucky if they could settle within the policy limits which were quite high.

Upon arriving in the southern California town, the claimant was driven directly to a sports stadium, not a football-field type of stadium but a closed building with seating ranged around a square stage-like structure in the middle. What could it be? Why, it was a wrestling ring! They went to a wrestling arena. Well, why not. They guy needed some entertainment. It is not much fun sitting at home all day long. No television! So, the investigator hurried to gain entrance and attempt to place himself in position to watch the claimant without being noticed himself. He needn't have bothered to worry about it. The claimant was not there as a spectator. The undercover investigator shot a lot of movie film that day of the claimant in two preliminary bouts and one elimination bout!

Anti-Climax -

The following week, at a meeting in the office of the claimant's lawyer, a modest settlement agreement was reached after viewing the very informative and entertaining movies acquired by the under cover investigator. The tide sometimes turns against claimants and plaintiffs in favor of the insurance companies. Many times it is the result of covert investigations by professionals hired especially for the purpose of catching people trying to defraud an insurance company out of money. If you have any idea of fooling the insurance company, its adjuster and perhaps the defense lawyer as well, at least have the good sense to realize that you may be under surveillance. Video cameras are relatively inexpensive now and video tape is cheap. Most field adjusters own them and know how to use them effectively to find out what their claimants are up to.

Sitting on a stakeout is often boring and non-productive. But when you get something good on a phony claimant, it makes all the waiting and the non-productive surveillances worth the effort. And surveillance activity is not restricted to sitting around waiting to catch the claimant playing football or working around the yard. That telephone call you got last night, was it really a neighbor trying to find a lost article on your roof? Or was it an adjuster or investigator hired by the adjuster to find out if you knew what was on your roof? Was that pretty girl who smiled at you yesterday at the washateria really interested in you or was she interested in your health? Or how about the shoe salesman who kept asking you to get up and walk across the store and back four times in order to see if the shoe really fit or was he trying to see if the shoe really fits? You probably thought he was admiring your legs!

The reports such operatives turn in to the insurance companies can turn your promising claim into regret very suddenly. Well, I can't tell you what to do. I will not suggest that you try to fabricate an injury in order to collect insurance money. Neither will I tell you to fake it while out shopping to make your real injury seem worse than it really is. On the other hand, it is important for you to be aware of the covert activities of insurance investigators. This is especially true if your injuries are severe and/or your claim settlement demand is very high. Other things can trigger an undercover investigation such as inconsistencies in your version of the accident, or improbable injuries in relation to the kind and severity of impact or type of accident. They may be watching you.

If your injuries are real. If your claim is legitimate. If your demands are realistic. If your attitude toward the adjuster has been cordial and healthy, you probably have nothing to worry about. But it still won't hurt to keep a sharp eye out and ears open to look back in order to see if you are being checked out by the insurance company.

Watch Your Mouth!

What you say can make a difference as well. As soon as the sounds of the collision begin to die down, someone begins talking about the accident. Someone will continue to talk about it for many years following the event. Though comments made after settlement may not matter, any thing said prior to settlement can have serious consequences on the closing of the claim. Perhaps the worst statement which can be made by a driver involved in an automobile accident is any statement he might make immediately following the accident. Such statements are called *res gestae* statements. The law recognizes such remarks, if made at the scene of the accident immediately following the event, as admissible evidence in a law suit. Normally, so-called hearsay evidence cannot be used in court, but the rule has been modified to allow some hearsay if the talking was done right after the collision happened.

Let me try to demonstrate. Say that following an accident, you get out of your car and say, "Gee, I'm sorry. I didn't even see you!" The other driver, his passengers or any witness who might have heard you say those words could later testify that you were heard making such a remark. Those words could then be used against you in determining fault in the cause of the collision. Even if the other side couldn't prove you guilty of any negligence at all, a jury or a judge could consider that careless remark you made to reach the decision that you caused the accident.

There might not even have been any reason for you to have seen the other party. The accident may truly have been the other fellow's fault. You could, nevertheless, have your claim denied or even be made to pay the other claim as well because of what might have otherwise been an innocent and non-relevant comment. I hope you will not get involved in any lawsuits, they are dangerous to your health and wealth. I hope you never get involved with any lawyer beyond a social relationship. So why am I so worked up over res gestae? I am concerned about your running off at the mouth in a way which may seriously limit your ability to collect insurance money without a lawyer.

Recently, after having been told so for many years, I finally learned that the exact words a person uses DO make a difference. In the past, to me words were only crude tools which one used carelessly and haphazardly. I always assumed that those hearing my words would <u>understand</u> whether I took the time to be precise or not. It was not ever true and I regret the many years it took me to learn it. Your understanding of the meaning of a word or phrase may be drastically different than mine. If, for example, you ask me which movie I would like to see, and I answer, "I don't care," how will you perceive that response? Will you think that I am trying to let you pick the movie? Or will you think that going to a movie is not important to me? Or will you even think that maybe I don't want to see a movie at all. Many would understand my answer to mean that I had no interest in them!

A much better answer might be, "I don't have a strong feeling for either movie, but I would like very much to see one of them. Tell you what, why don't you pick. We'll see the movie you like best." A thoughtful and complete answer. An answer which shows how I really feel about the movies and shows my concern for you and your wishes. Better yet, why could I not have simply said, “I like this one best. What do you think?” THE WORDS YOU USE DO MAKE A DIFFERENCE.

If when waking up in the morning, you ask yourself, “Why do I have to get up today?”, your very resourceful brain will find an answer. It may give you a strong reason for staying in bed. How much better your day might go, if upon waking, you asked yourself, “What wonderful things are going to happen to me today?” You might come up with the best reason ever for getting up and enjoying your life. The words you use, even when having a conversation with yourself, do make a difference. Your own words can have a profound effect on how you feel about yourself and the world around you.

That being true, how much effect do you think your words might have on an insurance adjuster when trying to evaluate your claim? The first rule should always be, “Don’t admit to doing anything which caused the accident.” Don’t do it at the accident scene and don’t do it later when giving a statement or when discussing the claim with anyone. Don’t make foolish accusations against the other driver, the witnesses to the accident or the adjuster. Think of all the people involved in the accident or the processing of the claim as human beings. Human beings with sensitive feelings. People who might be offended by some careless remark you might make. Think things through. Plan what you want to say and what points you want to make before you begin to talk. Keep your primary goal in mind: Collecting insurance money without a lawyer. Make every thing you say support and work toward that end.

Although you may not fully understand why I’m telling you these things at this point, you should know that not only may people be watching you, but they are always listening to you. While you may think it quite funny when you tell a friend that you are in the process of “sticking it to the insurance company,” the only one who laughs may be the adjuster when he denies your claim. Friends and acquaintances get angry at each other from time to time. Those intimate conversations, those friendly admissions of guilt can, in bad times, be repeated by an angry friend to the insurance adjuster. And it can seriously damage your efforts to maximize your insurance recovery.

It is not only friends and relatives who may be listening. Professionals hired to find out the truth about your injuries, your disabilities and the facts of the accident may be listening as well. Perhaps you are not aware of all the modern listening devices on the market today. There is electronic eavesdropping equipment built so compactly that a person can carry it around and you would never see it. They could be standing many yards away from you and yet hear every word you say clearly. They can park across the street from your home or office and listen to your very private phone calls without you knowing it. And if you use a cellular telephone, forget privacy, for every word you say is going out on radio waves which can be heard by anyone with a radio receiver tuned to the right frequency.

Run A Tight Ship -

Well, I know, this all sounds very paranoiac, but it points up the need for you to clean up your act. If you are going to make money at this, you need to learn how to do it right. And learning how and when to keep your mouth shut, and learning how to say only the right things at the right time is important to your success. Remember. People are watching. People are listening. And you are the person in control. Don't give that control over to someone whose job it might be to see to it that you collect nothing for your efforts. They are out there saying, "Peek-a-boo, I seeee you, and I'm listening, too!"

And, your insurance adjuster will be listening as well, especially if you agree to give him a *statement* of any kind. Statement, in insurance claimese means, a semi-formal account of the facts of the accident and the consequences thereof. Statements may be taken in writing. They may be typewritten. They may be recorded. If recorded, the recording may be on any of a number of types and sizes of plastic tape. The recording may be done in person, that is, in your presence, or they may be done while speaking with you by telephone. *In-person* recorded statements or *telephone recorded* statements are both legal. Although the adjuster <u>should</u> <u>always</u> ask your permission before recording a conversation with you, he doesn't have to. I know of no state in which a person cannot legally record his own telephone conversations with other folks without telling them their talk is being recorded.

The adjuster will call you on the telephone. He will tell you that he needs to take a statement from you. He will tell you that it can be done on the telephone. He may explain that in order for you to have consideration given to your claim for payment, you must give him a statement. HOLD IT! That last is not true. You don't have to give a statement to anyone in order to get them to consider a claim you are making. The only time you can be required to give a statement to anyone about anything, is if a judge in some court orders you to do it. And sometimes, you can't even be forced to do it then.

It is true, however, that if you want the adjuster to be kindly disposed toward paying your claim, you may want to give him a statement. The adjuster must find out the facts of the accident. He is charged with finding out what happened. He must learn why the accident happened as well as how. He must find out about damage to the vehicles, injuries, witnesses and so on. Since you were there, he will want to have your version of the events leading up to and following the collision. This might be a good place to try to explain just what the adjuster's job is.

An adjuster is the delivery man of the insurance company. He is the one who will deliver the product the insurance company sold to its policyholder. He must find out what happened and why. He must find out all of the consequences of those events, making a series of decisions along the way as to *coverage, liability, value* and *settlement.* In short, the adjuster's job is to reduce the accumulated events surrounding an accident to dollars and cents. To pay or not to pay. To deny or not to deny. And how much to pay.

The adjuster must determine if there is coverage for a loss. That means checking the policy to match its provisions with all the facts to see if it really applies to the claims which are being presented. Once coverage has been established, the adjuster then must find out if his policyholder caused the accident. If so, he must then decide who is deserving of payment and how much to pay them. After making all those decisions, the adjuster must then convince all the claimants to accept the amount of money he thinks they have coming to them. That is something which is much easier said than done.

However, before the adjuster can begin this heroic but friendly persuasion, he must first get settlement authority from the insurance company. All his facts must be in order. He must prove there is coverage. He must present a strong, understandable analysis of the facts to convince the insurance company that there is liability. That is, they must pay the claimant some money. And finally, he is faced with the task of getting the insurance company to agree with his evaluation of the claim and extend settlement authority in the amount of money he thinks is necessary to buy a release from the claimant. If he succeeds in all of that, he can then approach the claimant and begin settlement *negotiations*.

To Talk Or Not To Talk -

The adjuster's starting point is your statement. He will need for you to tell him what happened. Remember all those facts I told you to write down? The adjuster wants them all. He will, of course, get a statement from his policyholder as well. He will also interview any passengers in the insured car. He will get statements from any witnesses to the accident. He may already know more than you do about the accident, but he will still need your statement. Should you give it to him?

To me, that is an easy question to answer. I think you should give the adjuster a statement. Many claimant's attorneys, as we call them, refuse to allow their clients to give statements to adjusters. They usually say, "It is not our policy to allow statements." They usually add, "When are you going to pay my client's claim?" (Thinking of course that we are stupid and will just hand over the money.) But, I've often said that if I were a plaintiff attorney representing personal injury clients, I would allow them to give statements to adjusters in almost all cases. The few I would not allow would be the cases where the claim would surely be denied if a statement were given. I might hesitate to allow a statement in any case where I was aware of attempted fraud on the part of my client. But in all other cases, I think I would tell the claimant to give the adjuster a statement.

I, as an attorney, would probably sit in on the interview or at least have a *paralegal*, that is an assistant who may or may not be a trained attorney, sit in on it, but I would allow it. Statements given to adjusters do more to speed along the investigation and bring them to the payment of money than any thing else I know. Get the facts out in the open and then begin arguing about them. That is the way to get claims settled. Otherwise, it is almost like blackmail. By refusing to allow statements, the lawyers are saying to the adjusters that no proper investigation will be allowed. That the lawyer will make threats of a lawsuit, manufacture his own "settlement package" and demand payment - on his terms!

But should you give a statement? I don't know. If you have nothing to hide, why not give a statement? If there is something about the accident or your claim which may harm your chances of recovery, don't say it. You can decline to answer any particular question you don't wish to answer. You can always say that you don't remember. I don't think you should lie. But, you can withhold any fact you wish. You may even say to the adjuster, "I don't like the way you asked that question, therefore I'm not going to answer it, but go on with the rest of your questions." If the adjuster should be foolish enough to press you on any such point, tell him that the interview will be terminated if he doesn't respect your wishes.

And if you are to succeed in collecting insurance money, do not tell the insurance adjuster anything which will clearly give him something with which to avoid paying you. You have all the facts. You have a chance to review them. Analyze them for yourself. Figuring out who owes who money is usually just a matter of common sense, anyway. Keep in mind that adjusters, regardless of what you think, want to pay claims. That is their job. I don't mean they want to pay claims they don't owe. But most claims brought to an adjuster are claims which they may or probably owe. The reason? Most people know that when the accident is their fault, they are not entitled to collect anything and they don't make claims.

Give Credit Where Credit Is Due -

Even when the claim is a doubtful one, who better to help you figure it out than an experienced insurance adjuster? If you work with the adjuster on questionable cases, the adjuster will probably wind up paying you something anyway, just to keep you from hiring a lawyer. Adjusters want to close claim files. Lawyers want to keep the files open as long as possible to justify what you are going to pay them for handling it for you. There is usually no rush to settle a claim by the attorney since he already has an office full of claims now which will be settling on a regular basis while your claim ages in the file cabinet.

In short, I think you should give the adjuster a statement. Otherwise, collecting insurance money without a lawyer becomes very difficult indeed. Use your head. Don't say anything foolish and keep your answers as short as possible. DO NOT VOLUNTEER ANY INFORMATION TO THE ADJUSTER! If the adjuster doesn't ask for it, don't give it to him. If a question can be answered with a yes or a no, keep it to one of those two words. Don't add color and excitement to your story, it will only hurt you. Don't try to explain anything unless the adjuster asks for an explanation. If he does, act like you're puzzled that he doesn't understand the answer you've already given. Make him drag the story out of you. Not by refusing to answer, but by keeping your answers as short as possible and letting the adjuster find his own way through the maze of the interrogation.

A good adjuster will ask at the end of a statement if there is anything you wish to add to your remarks. If he does, always ask him how soon you will be able to collect some money on your claim. You can put the adjuster on the spot that way. If he is harboring some idea of not paying your claim, get it out in the open. If you can, talk about it while the recorder is still turned on. Mention the word insurance as often as you reasonably and sensibly can during the statement. The mention of insurance during a statement can render the statement useless in court. <u>While the recorder is still turned on</u>, always ask for the adjuster to give you a copy of the statement tape and a copy of any transcription of the statement into typed or written form. The adjuster must give you a copy. Saying it on the tape will provide proof that you asked for it in the event the adjuster does not give you a copy. Believe me, it will be an extremely embarrassed adjuster who must admit to the claim manager that he failed to give you a copy of your statement in the face of your proof that you asked for one.

A Tape Recording Of Your Own -

If you really want to do it right, go to Radio Shack and buy a telephone tap. Plug your own cassette recorder into it and record the conversation right along with the adjuster. You don't even need to tell the adjuster that you are recording it. And while you're at it, you might as well know that the adjuster may be recording every conversation he has with you, not just during the statement. Regard every discussion you have with the adjuster as one which is probably being recorded. If you bought that telephone tap, use it every time you talk to the adjuster. Keep track of what he says as well as what you say. You may find the tapes to be very useful when you get down to talking about money.

What did I say? The words you say do make a difference! The words the adjuster says can make a difference as well. They can sometimes come back and bite the adjuster in the you- know-where. Be discreet. Be careful. Be honest. Be smart. The world is watching and listening.
Your money depends on it.

13 How Much Is That Doggy In The Window?

Your claim may be worth a buzillion dollars or it may be worth nothing! How do you like that? I'm trying to establish the outside parameters within which you must work to find out how much money you may be able to collect. All adjusters are faced with the same task each time they begin the evaluation process of a claim. A claim may not have any value at all. On the other hand, it may have enormous potential. Exactly how much each individual claim is worth depends upon all the factors we've already discussed. The value is based on *damages*.

A well-known dictionary of legal terminology says that **DAMAGES** means a pecuniary compensation or indemnity, which may be recovered in the courts by any person who has suffered loss, detriment, or injury, whether to his person, property, or rights, through the unlawful act or omission or negligence of another. Shall I translate? Damages means an amount of money which can be collected by someone who has been hurt in some way by the bad conduct of another person.

After defining DAMAGES, the law dictionary then goes on to define 34 different kinds of damages! Many of them are similar to each other. Some are vague and have no place in our discussion. You have already read in this book about the kinds of damages the insurance company is going to pay you. They are *special* damages and *general* damages. You will be able to collect money for your actual damages. The damages may consist of compensatory amounts of money and consequential amounts of money. Compensatory means, you get paid for exactly what you can prove you lost in money. Consequential payments are made for those things which result indirectly or as a consequence of the compensatory items.

Think of them in only two groups. Special damages are the things you can prove with bills, receipts and estimates. General damages are the things which result from special damages. This is a short hand way of looking at them, but it will get you what you want. In the first group, hard evidence is all you need to show how much you have coming to you. But, you will need your powers of persuasion to convince the adjuster of the items in the second group.

Is the loss covered?

The first question which must be answered in attempting to place a value on any claim is the question of coverage. Is the loss covered by the insurance policy? There are many and varied types of issues which may be involved in answering that question. It will probably be of no concern to you. If it should become a problem, you will learn about it without effort on your part. The adjuster will tell you about any questions concerning coverage. If nothing is said, forget this item. You see, if there is no coverage, the adjuster will tell you and you must either forget your claim or attempt to collect directly from the person who harmed you.

There are cases, where the adjuster is handling the file *under reservation of rights*. This means that there may not be coverage, but the company hasn't made its collective mind up yet. In some of these, the adjuster may still work out something with you on a nominal or nuisance value basis. But if there is coverage, you can go on to the next item.

Liability - Do you have anything coming?

Everything depends on the *evidence*. You can talk to the adjuster all day long and get no where if you have no evidence. Evidence is the proof that the accident happened, that you were injured and that it was that other guy's fault. It includes all those papers and reports you were asked to collect. The receipts, bills, estimates, opinions and reports which should by now be bulging the sides of that grocery sack, make up the evidence. And make no bones about it, your success or failure in collecting insurance money with or without a lawyer depends entirely on the evidence.

It is as true out of court as it is in court. The difference being only in the person you must convince. The adjuster. He is your judge without powers and your jury by consent. Show him valid evidence in support of your claim and your chances are better than 50 percent that he will agree to pay you the major portion of your damages. That can be true even in a fifty-fifty case - **IF**, you do a good job of persuading the adjuster that his policyholder's best interests and those of the insurance company would best be served by a settlement rather than a lawsuit. By the way, you probably don't want to let the adjuster know you have been reading this book, he may scoff at your threats to hire a lawyer.

The question of liability depends upon a thing called, *the facts of the accident*. The details of how, when, where and why you were damaged will determine if there is any *liability* for the accident. All those details you remembered and dutifully wrote down for yourself will show whether someone owes you money damages or not. The possibilities are few. One, you don't have anything coming to you because there is no liability for the accident. Two, maybe you have something coming and maybe not. Three, you definitely deserve to get paid for your damages. No liability, questionable liability and clear liability.

No Liability - You get nothing!

If there is no liability, your only hope is to talk the adjuster into paying you something for the nuisance value of your claim. Nuisance value is akin to extortion. You threaten to make trouble for the insurance company if you don't get paid. The insurance company decides to pay you a small amount of money to get you to go away and leave them alone. You believe that a bird in the hand is better than going home with nothing and accept whatever the offer. They pay you a very small amount in relation to your actual damages and everybody goes home almost happy.

Questionable Liability - Well, we'll see.

When some of the facts suggest the other driver is at fault and some of the facts suggest that you are at fault, you have a bit of a problem. Such cases can sometimes be so evenly matched that adjusters call them *swearing contests.* You swear that you're right and the other guy swears that he is right. Whoever swears the best, wins! (But if you get caught cussing, that's a foul.) These are the cases in which your negotiation skills may be put to a very important test. The mere fact that things are not clearly on your side, does not necessarily mean, you get nothing. It may only result in reducing the final amount you are able to extract from the adjuster.

When the conversation about liability turns doubtful, you will begin to hear about *contributory negligence* or *comparative negligence.* Contributory negligence is a term used to describe anything you might have done which when added to the other fellow's negligence helped cause your damages. In such cases, the money you collect can be reduced or eliminated due to any contributory negligence on your part.

For example, you are driving down the street listening to the stereo in your car. You are not speeding, but traveling at a reasonable and safe speed. You look up to notice that the traffic signal light ahead is green for you. You proceed through the intersection, glancing down at your radio as you enter the cross street. At that time, a car coming along the side street ignores his red light and enters the intersection crashing into the side of your car. The investigation of the accident shows that at the time you approached the intersection, the other car was so close that you should have had a warning of clear and present danger. Remember, when you looked down at your radio? Had you not looked down, you would have seen the approaching car and might have been able to stop before crossing into its path.

Evidence to prove those facts would show you to have been contributorily negligent. Although the red-light-driver's insurance company will probably pay your claim, they may not pay it in full. Some areas have laws that say if you are guilty of any contributory negligence at all, your claim can be denied in full! But most have some modified form such as comparative negligence.

If your negligence is compared to the negligence of the other driver, you would be paid a percentage of your damages. Say the other driver was 80 percent at fault. You, then, would be judged to have been 20 percent at fault. You would, therefore be paid 80 percent of your damages. There is usually a limit of some kind. It would seem foolish to have the other guy pay you 80 percent and you pay him 20 percent! Some laws provide that if each driver is 50 percent at fault, nobody collects from anybody else. And some provide that if one driver is at least 51 percent at fault, he must pay the other and cannot collect any of his own damages.

You will most often face this problem when talking only about property damage claims. Whenever a bodily injury claim is involved, it is difficult to apply the rules of comparative negligence. It is too easy to simply raise the settlement demand on the bodily injury claim to cover any shortage. Outside of the court room, these matters are all negotiable.

Clear Liability - You got it made!

When the facts are clearly in your favor, you push as hard as you can to get as much as you can before signing a *release.* The release is what you are offering to sell to the insurance company. Technically, you are offering to sell them a legal right. The right is the right to sue them if you want. You can't actually sue the insurance company for the negligence of someone else. You sue the person who harmed you. But for the sake of ease in talking about it, let it sound as though you can sue the insurance company.

If you have a legal right of any kind, you may sell it if you wish. Your right to sue a wrong doer for hurting you can be sold. You get paid money and you give the insurance company a signed document which makes it impossible for you to ever sue the wrong doer later on for his bad conduct. The release is a contract and is of no value until you get the money in your hands. Staff field adjusters may pay you and take the release at the same time. Independent adjusters and telephone or office adjusters will probably ask you to sign the release first and they will mail the payment to you later. There are very practical reasons for that. Remember only that the release, signed or not, doesn't count at all until you get the money.

So you're past the question of who owes whom. And you think you've got some money coming. Now, you need to review the damage to your property and your injuries. The extent and severity of both will form the basis of the balance of your evaluation of the claim. All money damages flow from how seriously injured you were. The property damage, even if substantial, will have little to do with the total amount of money you will be able to collect for your bodily injuries. But you need to know how much the peoperty damage claim's worth. So, lets learn about finding the value of it first.

Your poor car!

The amount of money you can collect for the damage sustained by property you own and were using at the time of the accident depends upon written estimates and bills for substitute property. The most common piece of evidence to prove damages for your wrecked car is the repair estimate prepared by the adjuster, an appraiser or a body shop. But the real measure of damage is *before and after* value. Whatever your car was worth prior to the collision, it will surely be worth less after it is all bent up. Technically, you should have the value of the car appraised as it was prior to the accident, and then have it appraised in its wrecked condition after the collision. The difference in those two values is the measure of damage you are legally entitled to collect.

The Cost of Cars

But it is rarely done that way. By far, the most often used method of determining the value of a property damage claim, is the amount of the repair estimate. It takes less time. It is simpler. It's cheaper to have done. And most folks want their car back anyway. If the car cannot be repaired, there may not be any choice in the matter. In such cases the value of the car prior to the collision is established and you will be paid on that basis. No matter the after-value. The insurance company will take possession of your damaged vehicle and sell it as *salvage.* Actually, the salvage value is the after-collision value. But rather than subtracting the salvage value from the before-collision value and paying you the difference, the company will just pay you for your car as it was. That puts you in a position to go out and buy another car to replace your broken one.

If your old car is something you simply cannot live without and the insurance company has declared it to be a total loss, you will have the option of *retaining* the salvage. The adjuster will subtract the salvage value from the car's *actual cash value* prior to the accident and pay you the difference. You may then keep your old car and have it rebuilt, at your own expense. And now we must talk about actual cash value. Adjusters call it the ACV of a car.

Actual cash value takes into consideration a number of factors - usually two. The replacement cost of the vehicle new, less a reasonable amount of *depreciation.* The result is the car's actual cash value. Depreciation is how a car wears out. It includes normal wear and tear. It includes accumulated damage. It includes abuse. And it means *obsolescence. Obsolescence* is also the signs of your car growing old. It means that an older car is not as valuable as a new car.

When you buy a new car, do you know what happens the moment you drive it off of the car lot where you bought it? Well, whether you believe it or not, that brand spanking new car is worth about $1,000 less as you are driving it home than it did at the moment you bought it. If you still don't believe me, ask someone who has bought a new car and then tried to sell it soon after the purchase. It seems obvious. If a person can buy a new car from the showroom floor for a certain price, why would he pay as much for a similar car someone else has already been driving around? You wouldn't do it. Neither would most other people. Therefore, a vehicle begins going down in value, or depreciating, as soon as it is placed into service. That is obsolescence. It is the slowly diminishing value of property due solely to its age and its relationship with newer, similar items.

It is sometimes easier to understand depreciation if you think of an automobile tire. When you buy a tire, it has about 11/32nds of tread depth. As you begin to drive around on it, it begins to wear out. Soon it will have only 10/32nds of depth and then 9/32nds and 8 and 7 and 6 and so forth, until it has very little tread left. At that point the tire no longer has any value. Its value has been used up. Tire warranties provide that as the tire wears out, the most you can recover in case of a failure of the tire is a pro rata amount of the new tire cost. If a tire you bought sometime ago blows out due to a manufacturing defect, when it is 50 percent worn out, guess what? The tire manufacturer will allow you only half of the price of a new tire. They will replace the tire and charge you for the amount of tire you have already used.

Depreciation in insurance claims works the same way. Only it applies to everything, not just to tires. It applies to the paint, the upholstery, the battery <u>and</u> to the car as a whole. In addition to knowing what depreciation means, it is important to understand exactly what is meant by *New*. New means, the cost of replacing your car with a new car, similar to the old one, but at the price you would have to pay immediately following the accident. In other words, the replacement cost of the vehicle is the price you would have to pay today to get a "like kind and quality" car even though the actual car is three or four years old.

It sounds much harder than it really is. Suppose you own a five-year-old Ford Crown Victoria four-door sedan. Its actual cash value will be today's price of a new Ford Crown Victoria four-door sedan less five years of depreciation. You could even figure it on a mileage basis. In other words, simply deduct from the new car price, a certain amount of money for each mile on the car's odometer. Say, 28 cents per mile. If the car has 60,000 miles on it, the depreciation will amount to $16,800. If the car cost $22,000 new, its present ACV would be $5,200. If you look the car up in a used car price guide, you will see that it works out. The dispute you will have, of course, is the amount of depreciation per mile to be taken.

What usually happens is that the adjuster or appraiser look your car up in a standard book of values such as the National Automobile Dealer's Association's Used Car Price Guide, or NADA for short. The value shown there is used to approximate the value of your car. Those guide values are then compared to the price of cars available on the market. The comparable cars may be found on used car lots or advertised in the newspaper. The comparison car should be as close to being the same as your car as possible. Appearance, mechanical condition, wear and tear and mileage should all be taken into account. The result should be a price that represents the actual or real world value of the car damaged in the accident. That is the amount the adjuster will be willing to pay you. The NADA books are available in book stores for a modest price. You might find it useful to get a copy of the book current for your accident and learn how to check out the value of your car for yourself.

You may use this guide to appraising your vehicle whether it was damaged in a collision, burned or stolen. It is the same whether your insurance company will be paying for it or someone else's policy will pay. Of course, if you are making a claim for damage to your car against your own insurance company, you will have to suffer the pain of a *deductible.* Deductibles are a form of *co-insurance*. That is, you co-insure the car to the extent of your deductible along with your insurance company. Or to put it another way, you insure your own car up to the amount of your deductible. The insurance company insures the car for everything over that.

Usually the policy says that the company will pay for damage to your car only after the amount of damage exceeds the deductible. Deductibles are used to reduce the number of nuisance claims. These are very small claims which cost the insurance company more to process than is paid on the claim itself. The result is that you pay lower premiums when you buy the insurance, but you have to take some risk on yourself for small losses.

And beware of anyone suggesting that you have to pay the deductible to the insurance company. You pay your deductible to the body shop who repairs your car or you pay it to the seller when you buy a replacement car. DO NOT EVER PAY THE DEDUCTIBLE TO AN ADJUSTER OR APPRAISER. If any of them ever suggest that you should give the deductible to the adjuster or appraiser, report that information to the insurance company immediately.

Any other property damaged in the accident can be appraised by pricing a replacement item in a store. Remember they will expect to reduce the new cost by some amount of depreciation for the age, and wear and tear on the item. These may include clothing, luggage, cameras, telephones, tools or any other piece of personal property which might have been in the vehicle at the time of the accident. If any such property is damaged as a result of the accident, you are entitled to be reimbursed for those damages as well.

Don't forget Loss of Use. The cost of renting a substitute vehicle during the time your car is being repaired is then added to any payment for your car or other property in making up your entire property damage claim. Whatever that total comes to is what the adjuster should pay you if it is a case of clear liability.

Examples:

Assume the repair estimate on the damage to your vehicle amounts to $1,875.50. It took five days to repair the car. The car sat in a vehicle storage facility for four days before the appraiser looked at it. It took two more days for the adjuster to let you know you could move the car to have it repaired. Eleven days. Bear in mind, that the adjuster will not calculate the rental days that way. See Chapter seven. If your car was tied up, that is undriveable, for eleven days, you need to add up to six more days because of three intervening weekends. The number of car rental days is now 17, so calculate 17 days of car rental at $20 per day. The total is $340. Add that to the repair estimate to reach a total property damage claim of $2,215.50.

On the other hand, look at this set of facts. Your car is a total loss. It languishes in the storage lot for seven days before the appraiser sees the car. Now, the car is not a basket case. In other words, it is not immediately seen by the appraiser as a total loss but as a *border line* total loss. The appraiser makes his field notes while viewing the damaged car, but must go back to his office, check the NADA and look up comparable cars to see what your car is worth. He then must compare those figures with the probable cost of repairs. He must also obtain a salvage bid.

This process takes another three days. You are told at that time, that your car is a total loss, and the adjuster will get in touch with you. Another two days go by. You call to find out what's happening and are told the adjuster will call you back. Another day later, the adjuster calls to say that, indeed, your car is a total loss. He says the appraiser has decided that the car is worth $11,850. At that point in time, your property damage claim is worth $12,210. Eighteen days' loss of use plus the ACV of the car. If the adjuster cannot get your payment to you that same day, he should allow you a reasonable number of additional days of car rental value to give you an opportunity to replace your damaged vehicle.

One more. Your car has $580 in damage. It is still driveable. If you put the car in the body shop on Monday morning, it will be ready for you Wednesday morning. Three days' car rental at $20 per day plus $580 in repairs equals $640. That is all you have coming to you on the property damage portion of the claim.

All of these examples assumed a case of clear liability. There are many possible variations which we could discuss, but there simply isn't room and you would get sick of reading them if I tried to include them all. Make up some examples of your own for practice before you attempt to measure your own property damage claim. Now for what we've all been waiting for. How much *is* that doggie in the window?

14 HI HO, HI HO, IT'S OFF TO WORK YOU GO

You must decide how much your claim is worth. In this chapter, we are going to discuss how you can find out how much it is worth. It is a good idea for you to start out with a little organization. Decide where you are going to sit while figuring it out. Pick a table or desk top with enough room to spread everything out. If you have no desk, the kitchen or dining room table will do nicely. Make sure there is enough light for you to read. Some of the receipts may be carbons or poorly printed making them difficult to see in poor light. Get a comfortable chair. Put a small pillow in it, if you need to.

Gather up the tools you will need. Here is a partial list: Pencils or ballpoint pens. Plural because if you have trouble with one, you don't want to have to get up and go searching for a replacement. A pad of paper. I suggest a legal pad of yellow lined paper. A calculator. It doesn't have to be an expensive one, but it should have keys large enough for your fingers to fit without making mistakes by hitting the wrong keys. You will find that having a calculator which prints a paper tape, like a cash register receipt, will save you much writing. However, it will cost a bit more.

You will need some paper clips, to bundle like items together. Scotch tape to attach small items such as cash register receipts to a full sheet of paper for convenient reference. A stapler would be nice, but if you don't have one, don't worry about it. Some small, lightweight rubber bands to keep everything together and at least one manila file folder to keep everything in. It would be nice to have three or four. You could keep your property damage information in one, your special damage items in another and general damage information in the third. It is not necessary but might prove helpful, and they are inexpensive.

Ask your family, friends and loved ones to leave you alone for the time it takes to complete adding up the money you are going to collect from the insurance company. Don't misunderstand. It is not absolutely necessary for you to do this alone. If you have someone to help, fine. But as to anyone who is not going to help solve the problem, just remember that if they hang around, they will become a part of the problem, making it more difficult for you to do the job well. Now, go get that grocery sack, or the box or folder you have been saving all your documentation in. Bring it to the table or desk and begin. Oh, and as you begin, put some refreshments on the table for those moments of thirst, hunger or frustration.

Much of what you are about to read may seem obvious. You may wonder why I bother to tell you things which you would probably have thought of by yourself anyway. In response to that question, I can only tell you that it is important to do all the steps. Some of them are quite obvious and quite simple. Much of it is a matter of arithmetic. But in carefully detailing the basics, a solid, groundwork will be laid for the judgment matters which you must tackle later on.

Getting Down To Work -

The first step is to begin sorting out all the paper you've collected. Place the repair estimates, rental car bills, evaluation notes and any other items which relate only to the damage to your vehicle or other property in one stack. Separate the medical bills, including those from any hospital, ambulance service, doctor or other medical service, into another stack. Pick out any information you have acquired from any source about the facts of the accident, putting them in another stack. You should especially include your own notes about the accident and copies of any statements you have given. Stack the reports from the police, from doctors or from any other source into a separate pile, but sort them as to whether they apply to property damage or to bodily injury.

Anything which does not fit into one of those categories, keep in a miscellaneous stack. Now is a good time to use those extra manila folders, if you bought some. Place each stack of paper from each category into a separate folder and mark the folder accordingly. Use these terms: "Property Damage," "Bodily Injury," "Facts of Accident," "Reports," and "Miscellaneous." Of course, if you don't like those terms, you may use whatever words you please, but make them meaningful in relation to the task at hand. For example, you could use "car" for property damage, "Me" for bodily injury, "The wreck" for facts of accident and so on. Use whatever works for you.

If you don't have manila folders, use paper sacks or boxes. Use anything you have available, but keep each section of materials apart from the others. If you allow them to get mixed up, you will waste valuable time in resorting and looking for misplaced items. If you have accumulated a large quantity of materials, you may want to take a break at this point. Get up and walk around a bit. Get a drink of water if you didn't have a drink available at the table. Go to the bathroom, anything to get your body active for a while. Then return to your desk or other work area.

It is important for you to see some progress early. Therefore, I suggest you begin by adding up all the receipts, bills and other money items. Do the property damage items first. Sometimes it helps to make a list of the items as you go along. Such a list will become very useful to you later on. However, it is not absolutely necessary. You may be satisfied with attaching a calculator tape to each stack of items and making notes in the margin. But, remember, that you will need to refer back to these items frequently, and an itemized list is the best way to do that.

Start with your lined yellow pad. Place a heading on each sheet to identify which category or collection of items that sheet represents. Skip a line and write out identifying words for the first item of expense. Place the total of the money for that item to the right of the description and go to the next item. Continue until all the items in that category are listed. Then with your calculator add up all the items on the list and write the total at the bottom of the page. Then go to the next group of items or the next category and repeat the same procedure. Continue until all the cash items, receipts, bills, statements, invoices, estimates or appraisals have been listed and totals calculated.

As you complete the first portion, those items pertaining to the damage to your car, you should have a total of your property damage claim in front of you. It should include the amount of damage or loss sustained to the vehicle. It should include car rental expenses and loss sustained to any other property. The total is the amount of your property damage claim.

I should mention here that at this time you may have already collected the property damage portion of your claim. The insurance company may already have paid you for the damage to your car and possibly even the rental car expenses as well. You should still review the records now to fix in your mind an exact figure for your property damage claim. The amount of property damage could have an effect on the value of your bodily injury claim.

Complete the sorting, assembling, listing and totaling of all the categories. You should now have a total of the expenses you incurred as a result of the injuries sustained by your body. You should have a total and a breakdown of any wage loss or other income loss you suffered because of those injuries. Now go through the official reports.

Read To Understand -

Check the police accident report thoroughly. Check for anything obviously wrong, such as names, address, dates, times and so forth. The accident report will be relied on heavily by the adjuster in making a decision about liability. If there are details on the report which make your claim look bad, prepare to discuss those points with the adjuster. In the event there are glaring errors on the report, you might want to contact the investigating officer to find out why. Check to see if the facts of accident in the report support your version of how the accident happened. Pay attention to any tickets issued by the investigating officer. If you got a ticket, it is very important for you not to enter a guilty plea. Such a plea can be used against you and the adjuster will. Ask the clerk, you will be told that you can plead *no contest.* You will have to pay a fine, but the plea cannot be used against you later.

Look over all medical reports. Make sure that you understand what the report says. If you don't understand the report, call the doctor and get a full explanation. You are entitled to it. Find out if the reports accurately reflect what happened to you.

Are there any predictions in the reports as to what may happen to you in the future as a result of the injuries you sustained? Pay particular attention to any suggestion that you will need further medical treatment. Don't overlook any need for therapy of any kind, physical, mental or occupational. If those things are suggested by your doctor, keep in mind that they will cost you money. If you don't have estimates of the future cost, make yourself a written note to get the information at the next earliest opportunity.

Does the medical report say you will have any lingering disability of any kind? If it does, make special notes for yourself on those points. If you have any questions about it or if you do not understand the report, contact the doctor and get him to explain. Future disability can have an enormous effect on the amount of money you collect. The disability should be quantified, that is, it should be spelled out as to how much of a disability you will have. Will it be ten percent? Thirty percent? More? Less? Get it down to specific numbers. You will need them later on.

You may need another break by this time. Since I cannot tell how long this process will take you, I don't know if you can do all this at one sitting or not. If your injuries were severe or extensive - if your medical treatment was long or complicated, even if the injury was slight - you may need to break the procedure up into separate sessions. If so, just do as much as you can one day and get back to it again the following day. In most cases, you can do all that is necessary in an evening. If you have the time during the day, certainly it may be possible for you complete everything you need to do in a day. You should even be able to do the follow up work needed to fill in any gaps you may have left in your initial collection of information.

Okay, you are now refreshed and ready to have a go at it again. Summarize your findings on a single sheet of paper. List property damage, bodily injury, lost wages, future medical expenses, future lost wages and any other item of damage you may have. Keep the property damage portion of your claim separate from the injury portion. List the actual medical expenses together but keep any estimated future medical expenses in another group.

List the wage or income loss information separate from the injury stuff. And list the actual already lost income apart from any estimated future lost earnings. You should now have three major categories: property, medical expenses and wage loss information. You may also have future medical expense and future lost wages. Look at the figures for a while if you like, but don't do anything with them yet. Don't try to draw any conclusions as to the ultimate value of your claim at this time. At this time, you need to give some thought to who you are.

Examination Of A Naked Ape -

Who are you? But first, do you know who Desmond Morris is? Mr. Morris is the author of a book entitled *The Naked Ape.* It is about his study of humans. His approach was to study human beings as he would study any other animal. When you begin studying animal life, you need a name to refer to the animal by. Morris settled on Naked Ape. We belong to the ape family and we have no hair. At least not very much in comparison to the amount of hair apes have. So, if we can be considered Naked Apes, you are going to study one particular Naked Ape now.

Who are You? Are you a professional person? Are you a laborer? Do you operate your own business? Do you provide some critical service to the community? Are there others who depend upon your services for their health, safety or welfare? Are you unemployed? Do you live in a wealthy neighborhood or in the slums? How does you physical disability affect others? Do you have dependents? Will your family have food to eat? Will they be able to pay the rent or get to school? Can they survive if you become disabled? How will the adjuster view you as a person? Will he think you are an important person or a nobody?

Whether you like it or not, **all** of these things can have an effect on the value of your claim.

I know it doesn't sound fair, but that's the way it is. And claims evaluation works in peculiar ways. In some cases being wealthy can make your claim more valuable. In some, being poor can make your claim more valuable. Want to see how? A wealthy person making a claim against a poor person may be seen as greedy or vindictive. "Why," some may ask, "should this rich person try to get 'blood out of a turnip'", so to speak. On the other hand, some poor people are perceived as parasites trying to live off of the good fortune and hard work of others.

It is not so much how you feel about yourself, but how others might see you. The adjuster, like everyone else, will be judging you. He will be making decisions about the claim based on what kind of a person he thinks you are. As I have said before, these things do make a difference. So try to understand and be able to accurately see yourself as others see you. When you do, you will be in a better position to teach the adjuster that you are a human being. He may not see you that way. He may see you only as another claimant.

The adjuster needs to see you as somebody's son or daughter. He must begin to know you as a wife or husband. A father or mother. Sister, brother. Aunt, uncle, cousin, nephew, friend! He must hear the human side of your life. He cannot, under those circumstances, regard you as just another anything! He will see you, hear you and think of you as someone like himself and THAT is very important.

Public Relations -

However, who you are, insofar as claims evaluation is concerned, is important <u>only</u> in relationship to who the others are. Who is the person you are making a claim against? Consider who you are, compared to who that other person is. A rich man may fear the loss of his property, if the proceeds of the insurance policy get used up. A poor man could be covered by a high limits insurance policy, either his own or someone else's, such as his employer.

It is somewhat difficult to give examples. But suppose that you have been unemployed for the last three years. Suppose further that you have been living on welfare and the generosity of friends and neighbors. Say you smoke cigarettes and drink beer, both of which are expensive. You are able-bodied, that means you could get a job if you wanted one, but you just haven't gotten around to going to work. Further, assume that your injury is slight and the amount of damage to your car is minimal. There is reason to believe that the adjuster knows all about you. Under those circumstances, I suggest you make the best deal possible and take the money and run. Even with a lawyer, your life would have to go through a huge transformation for your claim to be successfully grown into high numbers.

Now you must be honest with yourself, but I want you to understand that in all cases, if you truly understand your circumstances, you can turn them to advantage when you begin dealing with the adjuster. That guy we were talking about above? The one who was out of work? If I were he, I would point out to the adjuster the fact that I have little to lose. I would remind him that I have plenty of time. My friends will keep me going as long as it takes. And if he doesn't work with me on this settlement, I <u>will</u> get a lawyer, do what he tells me to do and sit back and wait for the money to roll in.

A threat? Maybe. But what is the adjuster to do? Claims do not get better with age! They go stale and troublesome. As adjusters describe it, they begin to "grow hair on them." They only get worse. It is always in the adjuster's best interest to settle the claim as soon as possible. Believe me, with those facts, I would at least get more money than I really had coming to me.

What if I were a wealthy man? I would gently advise the adjuster that I really don't need the money, but I am upset over the accident and my injuries. I would explain how nice I am being to him by not having my personal attorney take this whole thing over and try to skin him and his lousy insurance company! I would suggest that he join me at my club in order that we could discuss my claim over a steak dinner. There is a way to use any walk of life, any financial circumstance, any degree of popularity or infamy to inflate the value of a personal injury claim.

What do you think the adjuster's reaction might be to a settlement demand made upon him by a known drug kingpin? I think he might like to settle that claim right away or find a new place to live and work! I don't want you to think that threats of violence or lawsuits will get you what you want. I want you to understand that the **fact** of these matters will, without doubt, influence the adjuster in his evaluation of your claim. You probably won't have to say anything to him about it. You only need to understand that the adjuster will know what kind of person you are and that knowledge will make a difference in his mind as to how much money your claim is worth.

Carefully consider who you are and what your life is like. Take a guess at how that will change the adjuster's thinking. Try to figure out how it might affect just how much he will think your claim is worth. Use that information, along with everything else, to make your claim worth as much as possible, even after you have added the numbers up.

Back To The Cash Register - I Mean, Calculator -

Find the total of your medical expenses. If the number is more than a hundred dollars or so, multiply the total by three. I don't care if the insurance companies don't agree, this is your claim, so do as I say. Multiply the total medical expenses by three. Add to that resulting figure the amount of your lost wages. If your doctor has predicted any future medical expenses, add those figures to the total you already have. Also add any anticipated future wage losses. The total, provided you have no permanent disability, should be the value of your bodily injury claim.

We'll get back to permanent disability later. For now, try an example. Your medical expenses total $285.23. You lost four days work at $64.00 per day. Your doctor has prescribed a course of physical therapy for you consisting of two sessions a week for the next six weeks in order for you to completely recover from your injuries. Two sessions per week at $75 per session is $150.00 per week. You will be doing it for the next six weeks for a total of $900.00. Each time you go for physical therapy, you will be forced to take off work for two hours, losing another $16.00 per day. Three days per week for six weeks will cause you to lose another $192.00 in wages.

Now add them all up:

Three times your medical expenses: 3 x $285.23 = $855.69

Lost wages: 4 x $64.00 = $256.00

Future medical expense: 2 x $ 75.00 = $150.00 per week

6 x $150.00 = $900.00

Future wage loss: 2 x 6 x $16.00 = $192.00.

Past medical expense x 3:		$ 855.69
Past wage loss	:	256.00
Future medicals	:	900.00
Future wages	:	192.00
Total Injury Claim	:	$2,203.69

In this case, ask for $3,500 and settle for $2,500 plus your property damage claim.

You can try it this way. A competent adjuster will catch you, but it may be worth a try to see if you can get away with it. It does work in some cases with some adjusters. Don't multiply the past medicals times three. Add everything up first and multiply the total by three.

Here's how it will look:

Past medical expenses:	$285.23
Past wage loss:	256.00
Future medicals:	900.00
Future wages:	192.00
Total:	$1,633.23

Now multiply that total by three: $1,633.23 x 3 = $4,899.69! Some difference, huh? Since you may not get away with it, be careful. Ask for $7,500.00. Step back in case the adjuster blows a cork, and wait for his response. If he doesn't unload on you right away, start negotiating as soon as he makes you any offer at all, and work toward accepting $5,000.00 plus your property damage in settlement of the claim. If you can get more, well and good, but do the best you can.

You can rest assured that your claim is worth at least $2,000.00 and maybe as much as $5,000.00 and that is all there is to it!

At least under that set of facts, that's all there is to it. Change the facts and the figures change, but not the way you go about adding it all up. There are, however, a number of other things which can raise the value of your claim far above the numbers alone. *Permanent disability* of any kind and any degree can make big, big differences!

If the doctor, in his report, says that you will be permanently disabled, the value of your claim goes up immediately. The degree of disability makes all the difference. Figuring disabilities can get confusing. But let me try to explain. There are lists, called *mortality tables*. Mortality tables show how long human beings will probably live. Here is how they work. The table will show that if a person was born in a certain year, based on what we now know, that person will probably live until a certain year in the future. A child born today is estimated to have a *life expectancy* of maybe 70 or 80 years. A person born in 1912 might only have been expected to live for about 60 years.

The point is that you can check to see how many years will pass before a person born during a certain time period is likely to die. If you know that person's current age, subtract his age from the number of years he would be expected to live and that is his remaining life expectancy. In short, guess at how many years you have left! If the doctor says you have a 10 percent permanent disability and the chances are that you will continue to live for another 50 years, you can figure out how much that disability is worth.

A ten percent disability times fifty years equals - what? Well, you see we don't have enough information yet. How much do you earn a year? How much will you earn in future years? You must decide how much you will earn each of your remaining years. Since we need an example, say that you will make $25,000 a year for the rest of your life. Now, we have already said that you have fifty years left and the doctor said you are going to have a ten percent disability for as long as you live. You see, that's what permanent disability means.

If you have a ten percent disability, we can assume that you may lose ten percent of your $25,000 each year, or $2,500. Since you are going to do that for the next fifty years, probably, your total loss over the rest of your life will be 50 x 2500 or $125,000! Okay, I know we're dealing in fairly small numbers when we say a disability of ten percent. It is unlikely that a court would ever grant much of a diminished earnings capacity on a ten percent disability, but that is how it works. You can tell the adjuster in such a case that your claim is worth up to as much as $125,000.00 more because of your disability.

A while ago, you had a claim that was worth between $2,000 and $5,000. Now we've got you up to between $127,000 and $130,000! I've got to tell you, this will not happen with numbers like this, but the principle is the same. You use the actual numbers of your claim, apply any disability given by the doctor and you can easily raise the value of your claim to more than most automobile insurance policies can pay.

If a person loses a *limb*, that is, a piece of your body such as a hand, arm, finger or leg, the numbers go up very rapidly and very high! The loss of the sight of one eye can result in collecting hundreds of thousands of dollars under the right circumstances.

It Hurts So Bad -

Well, what else? Think about it for a moment. What happens when a person get hurts? IT HURTS! It is painful to be injured. Injuries cause pain. When a person feels pain, they suffer.

When one has *pain* and *suffers*, that person has *pain and suffering*! I'm sure you know by now, Pain and Suffering are worth money. It's difficult to say how much pain and suffering are worth. It's really a guessing and negotiating game. Each person guesses how much pain and suffering is worth and then they argue about it until some agreement is reached. The amount of money they agree on is how much pain and suffering is worth.

I've often heard people say, "I wouldn't have gone through this for a million bucks!" Maybe not, but that does not mean that their pain and suffering is actually worth $1,000,000. But the value of pain and suffering is, in part, up to each individual depending upon how each reacts to pain. Some are tough as nails, others are wimps. The wimps may think they hurt the worst, but their claims may not be worth any more than the tough guy's claim is worth. But it does depend, to a large degree, on how each person reacts to the pain.

The amount and severity of the pain will determine how much the person has suffered. Once again, this is a matter of negotiation. In order to get the most you can out of any pain and suffering you experiences as a result of your injuries, make sure you can describe the pain in detail. Describe it in full, living color! Tell the adjuster how much it hurt. Tell him how long it hurt. Tell him about the pain medication you had to take. Tell him how rough it was on you when the pain pills wore off. Your medical reports will back you up. But even if your injury was slight, if it hurt, that pain and resulting suffering is still worth money. Make the best deal you can.

Saint Or Sinner?

You will recall that I said something about the facts of the accident having an effect on the value of your claim. I will give you some examples. If the driver of the other car was drunk or high on drugs when he ran into your car, your bodily injury claim goes up in value. If the car which ran into you while you were crossing the street was going 65 miles per hour in a 35 mile per hour speed zone, it adds dollars to your claim. It is not possible to put an exact dollar figure on how much the claim would be increased in value by these various acts, but you can use such information when talking to the adjuster to increase the amount of money you can collect.

And it really depends on just how bad the other driver's conduct was. Think about it on a scale of one to ten, with one being the lowest and ten the highest. Place a value on the conduct of the other driver in your honest and reasonable opinion. For each point from one to ten add ten percent to the value of your claim. For example, if the other driver's conduct was such that you think it was bad enough to get a value of two, add twenty percent to the value of your claim. A $2,000 claim would go up in value by $400 and a $5,000 claim would go up in value by $1,000.

If the conduct of the other driver was really horrible or disgusting or unbelievably stupid, you might want to give him a seven or eight. Add 70 or 80 percent to the claim. You will get a lot of resistance from the adjuster on this, but stick to your guns, because you are still giving the insurance company a break by not hiring a lawyer. In such a case, a lawyer might make a career out of this one. **You** probably wouldn't get any more money out of than you can by yourself, but the **lawyer** would make a **bundle**. That difference is why the insurance company ought to be grateful to you, whether they want to be or not. So, push the issue till you get what you want.

BE REASONABLE! Don't get greedy! Add up the numbers. Tack on the extras which you believe you can prove. Find the number you believe in and stick with it. Whatever that number is, it is the probable value of your bodily injury claim.

The beginning -

Let's take a look at a serious claim. Here are the facts of the accident. You are stopped at a red light. Traffic is passing across in front of you in both directions. Suddenly, you hear tires squealing. Later you may recall hearing crashing sounds before actually feeling the impact. Your body starts being pushed forward by the back of the car seat as your car is propelled forward by the impact. A large heavy sedan has just crashed into the rear of your car. As your car shoots forward, your body begins to catch up with the momentum and you are slung forward in your seat causing your seat belt to strain against your upper chest and shoulder. You don't even have time to see what is going on before a 2-1/2 ton dump truck loaded with gravel strikes the left front side of your car causing it to spin about like a clock. You are first whipped backward again and then sideways, as your body is thrown about the interior of the car. Glass is shattered. Metal crushed. Major members of the car's structure begin to twist and collapse. The front of your car crosses the right hand curb, now completely out of your control, and you smash into the front of a building on the corner. As your car collides with the building, you are thrown forward again, but this time the crumple shape of your car causes your head to strike the windshield in spite of the seat belt and your own warm blood begins running into your eyes making it impossible for you to see. One final whipping motion backward and you slump into what is left of your seat with the steering wheel now crammed against your chest and stomach! Just before you lose consciousness, you feel the sharp, searing flash of pain in your now broken, cut and crushed ankle and foot.

There are other noises, but you don't hear them for a while. When you begin to come out of it momentarily, you are aware of people trying to talk to you and it seems that someone may be trying to get you out of the car. Then the blackness closes in again, but not without the blast of pain screaming up your leg and into your back.

The noises continue, some of which you hear and some you don't. You are now drifting in and out of consciousness starkly aware of the pain which continues to dominate every sensation. When you waken, the panic starts. First fear. Then awareness that you can't move. Then it begins to feel as though you cannot breath. You gasp, but only feel the pain.

The firemen are now on the scene with the *Jaws Of Life* ripping the remains of your two year old car apart trying to get you out. You begin to feel sick at your stomach. The pain is worse but now steady. You are breathing but with difficulty. You still can't see. The blood still coming from your face and head has formed a blindfold through which you cannot see. After thirteen minutes of the mean sounds of the rescuer's equipment screeching in your ear the pain finally gets too great and you slip off into unconsciousness.

As the emergency medical team attempts to place you on a spinal board before moving you to the gurney, you return, and the pain is worse than before. Someone is wiping at your eyes with something wet and cold. You begin to see faces above you. Someone is asking if you know your name. You hear someone else say something about the *golden hour* and you wonder what that means. A plastic mask is placed over your mouth and nose. Needles are stuck in to your arms. You don't even care any more. And then, you begin to sleep. Not an unconsciousness like before, but sleep. The sleep brings relief with it and the pain finally begins to subside. You are in the ambulance, sedated, strapped down, asleep and pain free - for a while.

The middle -

An ambulance ride to the nearest trauma center, four hours in triage and emergency, six hours in surgery, two days in the surgical intensive care unit, back to surgery for two hours more, in recovery for eight hours, back to intensive care for ten days and into a semi-private hospital room for eight days and the doctor says you can go home! When you get home and the bills begin to arrive, you may find that you have been charged $4.96 for a band-aid and $2.00 for a Que-tip! Your hospital bill totals $28,496.23! The surgeon's charges total $2,870.00. The doctor only bills you for a paltry $1,200.00. And there are other bills: anesthesiologist, special nursing care, lung specialist, plastic surgeon (with estimates for future charges), radiologist, and numerous outside laboratory bills for various purposes. Altogether, your medical expenses total almost $38,000.00!

Now, you're sitting at home watching television as the TV Lawyers call adjusters liars and insurance companies thieves as they banter and caterwaul about how rich you will become if you will only call them for that FREE CONSULTATION. GET WHAT YOU HAVE COMING TO YOU! I'm always afraid of what that might really turn out to be. I may not want what I really have coming to me. Your car, you now know, is no longer among the living. It is dead. "A total loss," the appraiser said to you on the phone. You're still not getting out much, so the need for a car is not the most pressing thing in your life.

Your left foot and lower leg is still in a cast. The leg has healed, but the foot, with all those stainless steel pins holding it together, is still holding out! The soreness in your chest is about gone and your face looks almost normal. Except for the scars! The plastic surgeon has seen you once and is making plans to have you back again to discuss your future. It's been a month since the accident and you don't expect to be able to return to work, even on light duty, for another two weeks. You have time to think about the horror of the experience and the pain you endured. Fortunately, the human mind works in a very kind way by allowing the really terrible memories to fade rather quickly. Not that you forget the event, but you stop feeling the really bad things like grief and pain.

One thing I can tell you at this point is that even without including the damage to your car and forgetting about lost wages, your claim is already worth more than the vast majority of liability insurance policies cover! Do you need a lawyer? I still don't think so, unless you just really have a deep desire to give a large amount of money away. Most adjusters in this kind of a case will, very early, offer to pay the full amount of their policy to you. What you must do now is check out all the possible sources of insurance money available to you.

The first and most obvious is the automobile liability insurance policy held by the owner and/or driver of that large sedan which ran into the back of your car. If the driver of the car was not its owner and has insurance of his own, you may have two policies to go after - one on the car and one on the driver. There is a possibility that you could make claim against the owner or operator of the gravel truck depending upon the exact circumstances of why the truck hit you. For example the truck driver may have been speeding, or not watching where he was going. Speeding is called *improper and excessive rate of speed.* Not looking where you're going is called *failure to maintain proper lookout.*

If your car's policy has *Uninsured/underinsured Motorists* coverage, you can make a claim under your own policy for the liability of the owner/operator of the sedan which rear ended your car for anything those policies are unable to pay because low policy limits. If your auto policy includes PIP, you will have some source of revenue from that coverage. Maybe you carry *accidental death and specific disability* coverage under your own policy. You may even have a separate accident policy, or a travel accident policy which might provide some assistance.

And after all else is exhausted if you are still short on your financial recovery, you should consider how well off is the owners' and/or driver of the car which hit you from the rear. Perhaps, he owns property, or has a large sum of money in the bank or in investments. After all of the insurance money is used up, you can check these things out as well.

The end -

But let's look at a possible outcome for you. Say the car which hit you from behind has a liability policy with limits of 100/300/50. Remember, that means there is $100,000 available for injury to one person. Let's further assume that the dump truck has a commercial liability policy with limits of $500,000 combined a single limit and that the driver of the truck was speeding prior to the accident. And, to make it look somewhat better, the driver of the large sedan is a friend of the woman who owns the car. He has no driver's license and she knew it. His personal auto policy has minimum limits of $20,000 for one person.

Your claim could easily be worth $250,000.00 and maybe more, depending upon how long you will be off work, how bad your facial scarring turns out to be, the amount of your future medical expenses and any permanent disability you suffer because of the damage to your left foot. You have $100,000 assured from the car's policy. You have another $20,000 from the car's driver's policy. No doubt the truck's insurance company would be willing to chip in 20 percent of their policy limits to avoid a lawsuit. Result? You collect a$220,000.00 <u>without</u> any lawyer sharing the money with you.

Back to the beginning -

"Pipe dream," you say? Maybe so, but such things happen regularly in the real world. What if there were no insurance or very little insurance available? Maybe you would be in a very lot of financial trouble. Or maybe, just maybe, you might need a lawyer after all. But we'll get to that in Chapter 16.

The important thing to learn here is that if you gather all the information possible, organize it into sensible groups, add up the numbers and apply what you have learned about changing the numbers due to factors other than numbers, you will be able to place a value on your claim which an insurance adjuster will pay and you will be able to keep all the money for yourself.

15 GO FOR THE GOLD

The value of any claim is a combination of what you think the claim is worth and what the adjuster thinks the claim is worth. It happens, and much more often than you may think, that the adjuster's idea of what a claim is worth is the same as the claimant's idea of what the claim is worth. If it were possible for both you and the adjuster to be completely honest with each other at the outset of negotiations, you could probably both save a great deal of time. You could tell the adjuster what you think the claim is worth and the adjuster could tell you what he thinks the claim is worth. You could then make the slight adjustments which might be necessary to bring each person's expectations into agreement with the other and the claim would be settled.

But unfortunately, in our world, that is not possible. Because of a distrust bred between humans over hundreds, maybe even thousands of years, each party to a negotiation always thinks he must openly state a 'bargaining' figure which leaves room for negotiation. Likewise, each party keeps the real goal an utter secret until all issues have been fully resolved. Even then, neither side is likely to disclose what their actual intentions were. In polite society, we call it negotiation or bargaining. In the street world it is called dickering, arguing, haggling or even chiseling! Whatever, you call it, any time two people attempt to transact business with one another they must go through some process of negotiation.

The negotiation may be as simple as a sale in which the first asks, "How much?" The second person replies, "Three dollars." And the first person says, "I'll take it." Or the world famous classic,

"I'll show you mine if you'll show me yours!" From there the difficulty and complexity of negotiation increases at rates and measures which boggle the mind. At the upper end of the spectrum you will find labor unions bargaining with management over weeks and months to settle all issues. And you will see nations carrying out diplomatic overtures and responses, threats and counter threats and fighting wars in their attempts to resolve their differences with each other.

Marriages are made and destroyed through the process of negotiation. From, "Will you go out with me?" To, "Get the hell out of my life!" Friendship, courtship, marriage and divorce represent the epitome of negotiation including all its forms from dickering to haggling. But notice how unpleasant the term 'haggling' sounds. But, 'dickering', on the other hand, sounds so light-hearted and friendly. They are synonymous. It depends only upon your emotional opinion of the methods followed and the outcome achieved which causes you to call it one or the other.

I suppose you could say that attorneys negotiate and street vendors haggle. But in my view, they are both the same. You have a dispute. It is the desire of all parties in the dispute to settle it in some way. And the method you select is to talk about it. The result is negotiation. If we could be honest with each other, if we could trust one another, perhaps instead of negotiation we would experience communal problem resolution. But we can't! So we negotiate.

To Market, To Market . . .

You have something you wish to sell. I am interested in purchasing what you have to sell. You give me a price. We talk about it. You tell me how great the thing is, how valuable it is. I point out to you its flaws, and express regret that buying it might not be so great a deal after all. But, "At the price," you say, "it is such a bargain." And I, attempting to counter your praise of the thing, suggest that maybe I would be a bit more interested if the price were lower. "How much lower?" you ask. I try to avoid saying what I'm really prepared to pay and give you another figure, one much lower than my real offer. You then say that you can't let it go that cheap, but you would take another price. Not the price you are actually prepared to accept, but one much higher.

From there it is a matter of time and the number of moves necessary to close the gap down to a point where one side will give in or one will suggest "splitting the difference." The time it will take and the number of moves by each party depends on the size of the original difference between asking price and offering price. If at anytime either party refuses to change his last offer, the negotiation must end through either reaching agreement or terminating the discussion. For there is a time-honored rule in negotiation: "DO NOT EVER BID AGAINST YOURSELF!"

Let me give you a demonstration. You are the seller. I am the buyer. Your price is 50 dollars. I offer you 10 dollars. You say, "That is not enough." I say, "Well, how much would you sell for?" You reply, "I'll take 40 dollars." I say, "That is too much." You then say, "Okay, how about 35 dollars?" You just broke the rule. I now have the advantage over you. You have just reduced your price twice, first from 50 to 40 and then from 40 to 35 without a counter offer from me. All I said was, "That is too much."

Such a mistake would encourage me to stand on my 10-dollar offer, trying to get you to reduce your price further and further until I bought at a price much lower than I would have expected. In such a case I would have purchased it for a price lower than what you could have gotten for it with proper negotiating techniques. Insist on a tit-for-tat exchange each time there is movement. If there is no movement, hold your last position until your opponent changes his position. And if you find that he is not willing to make any change, break off the negotiation, unless you are prepared to seriously downgrade your expectations.

Let The Games Begin -

If it is your turn to move, MOVE! It's like checkers. When you play a game of checkers, you can't skip a move and wait for your opponent to beat himself! So, don't try it in the negotiation game. Oh, I suppose it is okay to *try* it, but don't be surprised if the adjuster reminds you that he has no intention of bidding against himself.

But how do you get started? How about starting out by simply picking up the telephone and calling your adjuster? It really is that simple. Ask the adjuster, "What do we need to do to get my claim settled?" Every adjuster should ask you for a settlement demand in order to open the negotiations. He will ask in some way, of you haven't already told him, whether you are prepared to settle your claim. If you say you are, he will then ask how much you want. Most people either truly do not know how much to ask for or else they are afraid to say what they want. The adjuster cannot make you an offer until he has some idea of what you are expecting. But try not to let the adjuster know what you are thinking.

If you think you are going to get big bucks and the claim value is quite low, what is the adjuster to say? If he offers you what the claim is really worth, you are going to be disappointed. You may even break off negotiations then and there. On the other hand, if the adjuster offers a high figure when you had only a low one in mind, he will have overpaid the claim, if you accept. Once you have given him a settlement demand, he will then know how to approach the discussions to bring your demand into line with his evaluation and/or the authority extended by his company.

If you open negotiations in that manner, you will have given the adjuster a distinct advantage. He will then know the parameters of the negotiation, and you won't. In other words, the adjuster will know your starting point or the upper limit of what you think the claim is worth. And, of course, he already knows his upper limit. At this point, you know nothing of the adjuster's thinking about the claim at all. If your starting point is higher than the adjuster's authority, he will be able to make an easy decision as to his chances of success in getting a reduction in your demand. On the other hand, if your starting point is lower than the adjuster's authority, he has it made! He now knows the claim is settled, it just a matter of how much lower can he get you to go before actually settling the claim.

You Go First, No You Go First, No You Go First -

You should always try to motivate the adjuster into making the first offer. You may or may not succeed, depending on the skill and experience of the adjuster. A competent adjuster, in making an opening offer, will keep the figure at or very close to your special damages. You may assume that he will pay more than that amount of money in order to settle your claim. It may seem at this point that you have the advantage. Probably not so. If you have paid attention to this book, you should know that the adjuster will at least offer you your specials. So without the adjuster saying anything, it is probably safe to assume what his lowest opening offer will be if the claim is one of clear liability.

Whether you can accurately predict what his opening offer will be or not, ask for it anyway. If his offer is higher than the amount of the special damages, he may have given you a clue as to how much he thinks the claim is worth. An opening offer which is substantially higher than the total of the special damages should tell you that the adjuster has a healthy respect for your claim and may be prepared to go quite a bit higher before reaching agreement. An opening offer at or close to the special damage total will tell you little more than what you might have already known or guessed. Such an offer may mean that the adjuster is being careful, or it may mean that he thinks the claim has little value over and above the specials.

Control Yourself, It's Later Than You Think -

Now you are faced with a decision. Should you make an opening demand at this point or not? Well, maybe the adjuster's offer is close to what you are willing to accept. If so, proceed with your demand and work out the difference. It shouldn't take long. However, if there is substantial difference in the adjuster's offer and the figure you hope to collect, delaying your opening demand for a while might be a good idea. In the real estate business, there is an old saying, "He who names a price first, loses." You do have to be careful.

But what do you do? If you go into any negotiation without a clear plan and goal in mind, you may begin to believe the other fellow's B.S. So, you start talking about your claim. In order to do that, you must be prepared. The preparations should have been made before meeting with the adjuster and that is what we are going to talk about now. The problem is one of unrealistic expectations.

There are two things I know of which cause more problems in our world than any other. They are *expecting too much* and *expecting too soon.* However the two are alike, there are differences. Expecting things too soon is called the desire for *immediate gratification.* Children and teenagers suffer most severely from this malady. It shows itself off by demanding that something be given, or done, or allowed, or made to happen - **RIGHT NOW!** Usually with no thought to the realities of time and the obstacles which may present themselves to achieving the results demanded.

It is no different in insurance claims. Things take time. If you accept that and work within the framework of the real world you will save yourself much pain and frustration. However much you would like the adjuster to "just do it now," it may not be possible. Work with the adjuster, but don't let him drag his feet. Ask him to establish the time limits. If he says he will get back to you, ask when. Ask for a specific day and a certain time of day. If he won't give you a clear answer, ask him why. Make him give you a definite commitment as to exactly when he will be getting back to you. Mark your calendar. Don't let him get by without contacting you as promised. If he fails, you call him. Point out his failure to do as he promised. Ask for results. Expect the adjuster to live up to his word. But within the framework of those agreements, be patient.

Unrealistic expectation is equally difficult to control. Although it may be unrealistic to expect the adjuster to get something done for you sooner, the expectations I'm most concerned about here are the expectations you may have concerning the amount of insurance money you are going to collect. You must be practical. You must be realistic. You must be careful. Gather your data regularly, completely and on a timely basis. Make an honest attempt to find out what your claim may really be worth and pay no attention whatsoever to the headlines in the newspapers or on television reporting that someone got umteen zillion dollars for their broken pinky.

It is your claim we are talking about here, not someone else's. The value of your claim depends on the facts of your accident, the facts of your injuries and the consequences of those facts on your life. If you carefully, accurately and realistically appraise the value of your claim, you can take that dollar figure into your negotiating sessions with the adjuster with confidence and a great probability of success in your future. Realistic expectations and patient acceptance of the time required to bring your claim to a conclusion will make you strong. There is no better way to enter any bargaining session.

Did'ja Ever Hear The One About The Farmer's Daughter?

So, you talk about your claim. Tell the adjuster what it has been like. Discuss the horror and panic of the accident itself. Describe the confusion and frustration of the accident investigation. Explain how your injuries limited and changed your life. Help him share with you the pain of your injuries and the dread you hold for the future. Remind him of the damages inflicted on your prized automobile. And make it clear to him that you expect to be fully compensated for all your damages. Use your own words, but make the adjuster understand that this is not just another claim he is discussing with you. Help him see that to you this claim is special and that you expect him to act accordingly.

Do not antagonize the adjuster. Keep all your discussions on warm and friendly terms. Let him feel that you regard him as a friend. One that is there to help you through and out of your difficulties. Difficulties that, after all, were caused by his insured. Maintain an air of innocence without sounding vindictive toward the adjuster's policyholder. And identify as early as possible all the outcomes which you and the adjuster hope to achieve through your negotiations.

For negotiation to succeed, there must be more than one winner. There cannot be a loser and a winner. That would make it a contest or a war. You don't want either. Find out how you can get what you want and allow the adjuster to get what he needs as well. The money you will be paid does not belong to the adjuster. He doesn't or shouldn't care about the money or how much of it he pays to you. Whether it be a small amount or large, the adjuster needs only to be able to justify the payment to his company.

Justification of claim payments is achieved with evidence. If the adjuster can provide sufficient information backed up with solid evidence, he can obtain settlement authority from his company in any amount up to the limits of the policy. Without them, he will get no authority at all. Even the adjusters who have discretionary settlement authority must prove why they spent the money. They can't just write out a check for any whimsical amount they choose without proving the need to the satisfaction of the company.

Seldom do adjusters undertake the handling of any claim file harboring the desire to avoid paying money on the claim. The need for payment of claims is the reason the adjuster has a job in the first place. And if the adjuster is competent and conscientious, although he will not want to pay a penny more than the claim is worth, he will sincerely want to pay every dollar that is due. Your job is to show him just how much is due TO YOU!

In the animal world, a great system of competition has been developed within species. Dogs will approach one another with a great show of aggression. They growl and menace one another. They snap and drool, baring their dangerously sharp teeth for their opponents to see. They circle around and around. They charge and stop. Move, shift, growl! But no biting! Little blood is ever drawn. Usually, one of the dogs will eventually lie down, roll over on his back and surrender. The victor will not pounce on his vanquished foe, ripping his throat apart. But he will stand over the exposed throat of his beaten enemy, growling and salivating, teeth bared, muscles almost rigid in neck, and back and leg. And then, after a moment of this ritualistic declaration of victory, he will drop his tail, relax and jauntily trot away.

The other dog? His life seemingly spared, may get up and actually trot along behind his new leader. They both knew the rules. They entered the negotiations aware of their own capacities and a realistic expectation as to the results of their encounter. And although one seemed to have lost, they both actually won. Each kept his life. Each kept his health. A relationship of seniority and rank was established without bloodshed. Balance was achieved giving a degree of safety and security to both animals. Humans do the same thing.

However, we do it much more clumsily and frequently with much pain and bloodshed. Humans more often than not leave their beaten enemies dead on the field of battle. It sometimes seems as though we just don't know when to stop. We act more aggressively and often go much beyond the needs of our goals to prove a point. In short, we almost always try to have a winner and a loser. Many times we attempt to have one winner and multiple losers. That should not be your goal.

You want to collect insurance money without a lawyer. If you push too hard, you may shove the adjuster into a defensive position from which he cannot escape. The result may be no settlement at all without going to court, or at least bringing lawyers into the contest with you. In most cases that will not be in your best interest. It has been reported in an audit of many of the nation's large, self-insured truck lines that, typically, settlement of accident claims are 30 percent higher when a lawyer is involved. If the lawyer gets a third off the top, and the size of the settlement is increased by only 30 percent by his involvement, where does that leave you? With less money.

Aha, another new term. Self-insured. Some companies, because of their size and the large number of claims they experience, elect to insure themselves instead of buying insurance from an insurance company. They usually set up claim departments of their own. They may use staff adjusters or hire independent adjusters. Insofar as the claim is concerned, there is little difference. In such a case, you would be dealing directly with the "wrong doer," instead of dealing with an insurance company on behalf of a wrong doer. Should you find yourself in that position, engage the adjuster the same as you would in any other case.

Say What?

In trying to persuade the adjuster to make an opening offer, you might try something like this: "You're the adjuster. You have the skill, knowledge and experience. I don't. I trust your judgment. What do you think? If you were me, what would you ask for in settlement of this claim?" An appeal such as this can be very seductive. The adjuster can hardly refuse to acknowledge the compliment and he is likely to respond to your very personal appeal for advice.

Be gracious and generous. Try to get what you want, but don't try to bludgeon the adjuster. He will happily pay you some money. The trick is to get him to pay you as much as you can without being unpleasant about it. Make your goal the successful collection of money with dignity and self-respect for both you and the adjuster. Keep in mind that the adjuster is somebody's son, probably someone's husband and there may be loving children waiting at home for their daddy. Don't mistreat him and don't try to emotionally beat him up. Get the adjuster to pay you a bunch of money! Help him be glad to do it, because you are such a reasonable person.

Thrust and parry, move and counter move.

As you start talking about the money, pay close attention to the moves that are made. Try an exercise. You start at 100. I will start at 25. If we negotiate in good faith and make regular moves, where will we end up? We should end up at 62 and ½. You can figure it out for yourself. It makes little difference about the starting numbers. Whatever the numbers are at the outset, you can quickly calculate where the middle will be. Your goal should be to settle somewhere in the upper half of that range. In the exercise we did above, you should try to move the negotiations upward, as soon as you can, to attempt a settlement in the area of 80. Avoid matching your opponent's moves dollar for dollar. If the adjuster comes up ten, you should go down five. If he offers an increase of 50, reduce your demand by 25 or less.

Pay attention. If the adjuster begins to match your smaller increments or worse tries to reduce his even further than yours, stop the negotiations for a while. When you begin again, raise your demand back up a notch or two. Impress on your opponent that you are going to control the moves if they are to move in his direction. He cannot afford to fight you. Remember, if this is a case of clear liability, he must pay you some money. It is only a question of how much. You have the advantage.

Since it is your advantage, you might consider throwing the adjuster a bone or two. Give him an extra reduction at a time when it seems as though he needs one. But remember to make up for it later by adjusting the reductions you make. He will probably not notice if you have laid the right groundwork by getting him to relax and think things are going his way.

If the adjuster seems to slow down in his moves, you slow down as well. If he speeds up, be careful. Don't let him trick you into a race. You will likely wind up 'splitting the difference' on a large gap in your bargaining. You can increase the pace of your offers but at a slower rate than that set by the adjuster. Stay ahead of him in your thinking and behind him in your moves.

I'll Meet'cha haf' way -

Sooner or later, one of you is going to suggest splitting the difference. Make sure that it is only a small difference that is being split. Otherwise, you will be losing money. If the adjuster suggests it, quickly and mentally analyze the size of the gap. If it is big in relation to the moves which have been occurring, do not agree to the split. If you are the one to suggest it, wait until the gap is small or until the split of a larger segment will move the settlement quickly to a much higher level. You should always be aware of the dangers involved in splitting the difference. The bigger the spread, the more probability there is to encounter deadlock! You should be prepared to walk away.

Should the negotiations be going badly, stop for a while. The pause could be for a short time, such as an hour, or it could be an interruption lasting a few days. But avoid continuing the bargaining if you are not getting the results you want. Use any excuse that comes to mind. Or better yet, have a planned excuse ready for use at a moment's notice. The idea is to disengage, retreat and reconsider. During the delay, go over the negotiations. Make some notes for yourself. Calculate where the negotiations were headed when you took the break. Develop a plan for restarting the negotiations.

Don't be afraid to restart the negotiations by telling the adjuster that you didn't like the way things were going the last time. Tell him that you don't think he realizes how much your claim is worth. Try to reopen the talks at a much higher level than before. If the adjuster tries to get you to start where you left off, tell him that was the problem before and it is no better now. Say to him, "I want to be fair." Remind him, "We should both feel good about the outcome of these talks and I know you want to be fair, too." Then, move him into a higher starting position and begin the process all over again.

Continue the talks until you reach a point where it is clear to you that you will reach the range of your desired settlement or until it is obvious the adjuster is unwilling to make the necessary movement to get to your goal. If the latter, you should stop the talks and go back to the drawing board, or kitchen table, whichever the case. You must find out what is wrong. Is your evaluation too high? If so, rethink your evaluation. Make adjustments which you think will help in reaching a satisfactory settlement and return to the bargaining table with a new plan in mind.

Back To The Salt Mines -

That plan should include the current state of the negotiations. Your last position. The adjuster's last position. To say it another way, what was your lowest demand and what was the adjuster's highest offer? What moves were made? Who moved last, you or the adjuster? Since you broke off the talks, you will have to make the opening move when you begin again. Therefore, your plan must include what you are going to say next and how you intend to get the adjuster's thinking closer to your own.

Give some thought to the adjuster. What kind of person is he? Based on your previous meetings, how did he act? What seemed to impress him the most? What impressed him the least? Was there some particular point which helped you a lot? If so, use that same point again. Nothing beats success but a copy of itself. And do your arithmetic again.

How much are you actually willing to accept? How far away from that sum are you? How much do you need to get the adjuster to move? Divide the difference up into small pieces and count the moves it will take to get you to where you want to be. Then decide on how much to open your next negotiation session with. Once you have worked out a new plan, believe in it. Approach your next encounter with the adjuster with total confidence. Assume that you are going to succeed!

With your new plan in mind, begin by asking the adjuster what it would take for his company to pay you what you think the claim is worth. Ask him straight out. "What do you need? What must I do to make it possible for you to pay me the amount I'm asking for?" Throw the ball into his court. Make him play!

Try this sample: Claimant says: "Mr. Adjuster, we are so close. Let's see. You're at 500 and I'm at 700. We've been at it for a month now, but we are <u>so</u> close. If the adjuster offers to split the difference, say to him, "So you're willing to pay me 600? And, I am at 700. Boy, we are **so** close. Let him offer to split the difference again. And respond with, "So, what you're saying is that you would pay me 650, right? And I'm at 700. Wow. We **are so close!**

Save yourself from the danger of overzealousness. If it appears that you will reach your goal, don't make the mistake of raising your desires. It can be very seductive to see your adversary moving into range of your sights. When you begin to smell blood, you may be tempted to press on for even more money. Don't do it. As the increments of movement get smaller and smaller, you may be reaching the end of the adjuster's string. Keep this in mind and don't lose what you've already gained reaching for more, especially if the adjuster is running out of money. If you can get what you set out for, take it graciously and enjoy your success.

You see, all during the negotiations, the adjuster knew what was going on as well as you. The settlement you were headed for will be as obvious to him as it was to you. Changing your goals at a late stage of the talks will be a clear signal to him to back off. It could jeopardize the entire transaction. The little gain you might achieve will not be worth the total breakdown of the talks, if it fails. Take what you can get and go home. If you've done your homework well, you will have gotten all you set out to get. And whether you know it now or not, the reward will be greater than just the money. You will experience the thrill of the successful conclusion of a plan you researched, engineered and executed, all by yourself. You are entitled to be proud!

16 Can't Get No - Satisfaction!

Well, how do you feel now? If you have actually been involved in a motor vehicle accident and worse, if you were injured in that accident, I fervently hope your injuries were not severe. I hope that everything has already worked out well for you and hope this book had a part in it. If you have not suffered the troubles of an automobile collision or bodily injuries from such an event, I hope that you will learn from this book what you will need to help a friend or relative or even yourself should fortune ever turn on you. As I said in the beginning, this book is intended to help people handle their own insurance claims without having to share the proceeds of any settlement with a lawyer.

But even more than that, it is hoped that the book will help you better understand the many problems associated with damage, injuries and claims arising out of vehicular accidents. Should you ever have need of a lawyer in such circumstances, perhaps the book will help you in your dealings with the attorney. For now, I assume that the accident is a fading distant memory and the pain of any injury has long since subsided. I want to believe that you successfully investigated, researched and evaluated your property damage and bodily injury claims. And, that you were able to successfully negotiate a substantial settlement with the insurance adjuster and that you were able to collect a bunch of insurance money, without a lawyer!

Most insurance claims are relatively small. The range is probably from about a$750.00 to around $5,000.00. Those are the claims which anyone can learn to handle on their own. Such claims should present little problem to the student of this book. Claims involving amounts over $5,000.00

bring slight additional difficulty until they approach the limits of an insurance policy. Presently, most are around $20,000.00. If the claim is valued at more than the policy limits of the policy under which the claim is being made or if the claim is for substantially higher sums of money, although I still believe this book will serve you well, prosecution of the claim becomes more complicated and time consuming. Well, what if it doesn't work? The subtitle of this chapter is: "What if?" What if it doesn't work out for you?

What if, in spite of your best efforts, in spite of your faithful study of the book and carefully doing everything it suggests, you are still unable to get the satisfaction from the insurance company you feel you deserve? What if your claim is so huge, or the issues so complicated that you simply can't do it for yourself? Well, maybe, just maybe, you need a lawyer.

There are issues which can overwhelm an ordinary untrained person. You may have been injured in an accident involving multiple wrong doers. There may be a number of insurance companies involved. There could be questions regarding coverage which would either prevent an insurance company from settling your claim or which might slow it down unreasonably. In those cases you might need to turn to an attorney for assistance.

Even if you use the book, even if you follow all the steps and are poised for a negotiating attack on the adjuster such as he has never seen before, you might want to pay a lawyer $50.00 for a consultation. The fee is modest and the attorney could review the summary of your claim and tell you if you are going in the right direction. You must be careful, for it would not be surprising to have a lawyer tell you that you've done it all wrong and that you need his services to *straighten it all out*!

But for many reasons, your case may be different, difficult or dopey. In that case, you could need an attorney. It is important to point out that men and women go to much trouble and expense to complete a legal education. It takes years and much, much money! Even after completing all the training, they still must take the much feared and unfairly maligned bar examination before the practice of law is permitted to them. The practice of law has such great importance in our lives.

We are a nation of laws. Our government is based upon the concept of the permanence of the law and the impermanence of the people who make and administer the law. It is our comfortable reliance on this concept that allows us to be free people. It makes liberty possible for all of us. And the people who are charged with the responsibility of untangling the legal problems we get ourselves into must be intelligent, resourceful and well trained. I wish I could add that not only are all lawyers intelligent, resourceful and well trained, that they are also moral people as well. Unfortunately that is not the case, just as it is not the case, that all doctors are moral folks and that all Indian chiefs are moral folks. So, when you think you need a lawyer, you must proceed with caution!

Needle In A Hay Stack -

How do you find a lawyer? To begin with, you look very carefully. I can tell you without reservation that there are some fine lawyers practicing law who will work hard for you and treat you fairly and with respect. I know and admire many attorneys. I have dealt with them for almost 35 years. They have faced me across many negotiation sessions and they have sat along side me, in court and out, protecting the interests of the insurance companies I represent. Some of them have looked after my best personal interests from time to time. Some of them became dear friends over the years.

That doesn't mean that I think you need a lawyer in every case! I still say to you that in most cases you can successfully collect scads of insurance money without lawyers! But I know that there will be times when you will need a lawyer. And when you need a lawyer, THERE IS NO SUBSTITUTE! To proceed on your own in any court other than city courts, Justice of the Peace courts or small claims courts is legal suicide! You may even find that in those lower courts, once legal action is begun, the services of an attorney can become invaluable.

So, okay, I give up. You may now need a lawyer. But, you must understand something about the fellowship of lawyers. The lawyers have one of the strongest unions in the entire world. It is called the Bar Association. Within that association, lawyers deal with each other on a basis different from any other known to mankind. And outside that association, it is difficult to attack a lawyer. They stand together. They protect one another. They will not "rat" on another lawyer. They will not testify against another lawyer, except under the most extreme circumstances.

And, outside of private conversations, they will not criticize another lawyer. This presents a problem to the person looking for a lawyer. *Who do you trust?* as Johnny Carson's old television show was called. The best source of general information about lawyers is the bar association. They have, of course, complete listings of all lawyers and they know which lawyers specialize in certain areas of the law. You may not find them very cooperative, however.

The next best bet is to go to your public library. There are a number of books which list lawyers everywhere. Lawyers in your town, in your state and across the nation. One is called *Martindale & Hubbell.* It is a rather large set of books, but you can learn a lot about lawyers, who they are, where they are and so forth. There are insurance publications, such as *Best's Recommended Insurance Attorneys* and others. Ask your librarian for assistance.

And once you have some names, it is a good idea to check them out further. Every court jurisdiction keeps a record of trials, usually called, *The Trial Reports.* This is small publication listing all the cases filed in the courts and brought to some kind of conclusion, either by trial to a verdict or by settlement between the parties. It can tell you whether a lawyer actually tries cases or whether he is an office lawyer instead of a court room lawyer. Many lawyers have no intention what-so-ever of trying a lawsuit. They make too much money settling claims to waste their time trying lawsuits!

Does He Or Doesn't He?

Some years ago, I had been talking to a lawyer about a claim for some time. During each of our conversations, he would manage to sneak in a threat. He would say, "You know, if we can't get some favorable movement, my client is going to force me to take further action. We may just have to file suit!" Those words are supposed to strike fear in the hearts of adjusters! Of course it never does, if the adjuster has been on the job more than two weeks. Tiring of these threats, one day I finally said, "Look, if you can even find out where the court house is, why don't you go ahead and file your lawsuit!" I knew, without any doubt, that he would never file a lawsuit, and HE NEVER DID!

After all, it was just a threat, and I knew it. Those lawyers collect big bucks from insurance companies without ever leaving their offices. They have no need for court rooms other than to use them to threaten people. You may need that kind of lawyer. Let me give you an example of such a situation. Assume that you have been dealing with an incompetent adjuster, of which there are, unfortunately, far too many. And since the adjuster doesn't know what he is doing, your claim is not being paid or it is not being paid fairly. Maybe the adjuster is not really stupid, but mean. Maybe he just likes to exercise his power by making insurance claimants jump through hoops to get their money.

In such a case, it should not be necessary to file a lawsuit to get your money. In fact, as I have said elsewhere in this book, you can take fix it yourself by eliminating that adjuster from the equation. Simply call the adjuster's supervisor or claim manager to let them know what's going on. And in extreme cases, don't hesitate to ask for the adjuster to be replaced. But if your patience has already worn out, an office lawyer might be just the person you need. On the other hand, if you need a trial lawyer, one who has the knowledge, skill and experience to represent you in court, you need to find one who not only knows where the court house is, but one who is familiar with the courts and comfortable in them.

There are two very practical sources for information about lawyers which I recommend. The first is to contact an insurance defense lawyer or his firm. The folks who work in the defense firms are familiar with the plaintiff lawyers in your area and can give you good advice about them. And while you are seeking this advice from a defense lawyer, check that lawyer out as well. Defense lawyers take plaintiff cases, too. And since many of them have heavy experience in insurance claim matters, you may find that one of them is the best to represent you against an insurance company. Realize, of course, that a lawyer will not take your case if it involves an insurance company he represents.

And finally, the best source I believe is to talk to your friends, your neighbors and your relatives. Ask them if they have had occasion to use a lawyer. Find out what they know, what their experiences have been with lawyers. You will be surprised at how many people have had dealings with lawyers. And all of them will have opinions! Some of those opinions will be quite strong and some of them may be unfairly critical of a particular lawyer. So you must talk to more than one person.

If you live in a small community, your selection may not be great. You may wind up using a general practitioner, a lawyer who is a legal *Jack of All Trades.* In larger communities, the selection will be greater. You will have more lawyers to choose from and you will likely find many people who know the lawyers and can give you good advice about them. When you find yourself in the large metropolitan areas, you have an abundance, Ye, an over abundance, of lawyers! And your task becomes much more difficult.

But still, within your neighborhood, you will find persons who have had experiences or know of someone who has and can tell you about a lawyer or two. But within this framework please pay attention to me now: TRY TO AVOID DEALING WITH A RUNNER! The runner is more concerned with lining his own pocket than in helping you. He may send you to an unscrupulous or even dishonest lawyer for the sole purpose of collecting a fee from the lawyer. You will, in such a case, be the subject of the lawyer's bounty to these modern day *bounty hunters*. And none of them will be interested in your problems or your well being.

If, once you have identified a lawyer you think you like, consider checking him out further with another lawyer and don't sign ANYTHING in the lawyer's office without reading it over carefully and thinking about it, at least overnight, before signing up. If the lawyer acts offended by your caution, run, don't walk, out of his office and find yourself another lawyer. There is an old saying: "If something is a good deal right now, it should still be a good deal tomorrow." If not, maybe it's not a good deal at all!

Lawyers, like salesmen, will try to get you to make a deal RIGHT THIS MINUTE! They do not want you thinking it over, for you might not come back. If they try to push you into something, you don't need them. There are plenty of them around, you certainly don't have to take the first one you meet. And even if you do like the first one you meet, check out some others anyway.

Performers, Pretenders And Paralegals -

But while we're talking about dealing with people at the law firm, you need to be aware of the possibility that the lawyer you have picked will not actually handle the claim for you himself. He may pass it on to a paralegal or legal assistant. That sophisticated sounding name could be another way of referring to his claim secretary, who may have been his receptionist only last week! Once your file has been given to a paralegal, no matter how well trained they may or may not be, you might never hear from the lawyer himself again in this lifetime!

The use of paralegals or legal assistants is a method lawyers use to maximize their volume. Theoretically, the lawyer will supervise or oversee the activities of the paralegal. All too often, however, the paralegal acts with total autonomy, making decisions which have deep consequences for your life without ever consulting with the actual attorney again. You are much better off dealing with a lawyer who personally handles your file himself. You will know quite early because all of your phone calls will be returned by someone other than the lawyer. And as your claim progresses, you will find that you never get to talk directly with the attorney

Unless you are satisfied with working with someone other than a lawyer to handle your claim or other legal matter, you may be just as well off taking care of it yourself. And the final step in checking lawyers out may surprise you.

ASK YOUR INSURANCE ADJUSTER ABOUT THE LAWYER! Say to him, for example, "You know, I am afraid I am going to need a lawyer to handle this for me. Can you recommend someone?" Give the adjuster a moment or two to stop choking before expecting an answer. Although a number of things could happen, most likely it will be one of two things. Either the adjuster will seriously discuss with you what he knows about the lawyer you have named or he will suggest a competent attorney he knows in response to your question, OR . . .

He may ask, "Why do you think you need a lawyer?" And you say, "Because we've been at this for some time now and we don't seem to be getting any closer to meeting my needs." You may find at that point a substantial change in the adjuster's approach to your claim, and you may find, surprise, surprise, that you don't need a lawyer to collect insurance money after all!

#

INDEX